Palladian Style
in Canadian Architecture

Nathalie Clerk

**Studies in Archaeology
Architecture and History**

**National Historic Parks and Sites Branch
Parks Canada
Environment Canada
1984**

©Minister of Supply and Services Canada 1984.

Available in Canada through authorized bookstore agents and other bookstores, or by mail from the Canadian Government Publishing Centre, Supply and Services Canada, Hull, Quebec, Canada K1A 0S9.

L'original française s'intitule **Le style palladien dans l'architecture au Canada** (no de catalogue R61-2/9-10F). En vente au Canada par l'entremise de nos agents libraires agréés et autres librairies, ou par la poste au Centre d'édition du gouvernement du Canada, Approvisionnements et Services Canada, Hull, Québec, Canada K1A 0S9.

Price Canada: $8.25
Price other countries: $9.90
Price subject to change without notice.

Catalogue No.: R61-2/9-10E
ISBN: 0-660-11530-1
ISSN: 0821-1027

Published under the authority
of the Minister of the Environment,
Ottawa, 1984.

Translation: Department of the Secretary of State
Editor: Paula Irving
Cover design: Louis D. Richard

The opinions expressed in this report are those of the author and not necessarily those of Environment Canada.

Parks Canada publishes the results of its research in archaeology, architecture and history. A list of titles is available from Research Publications, Parks Canada, 1600 Liverpool Court, Ottawa, Ontario K1A 1G2.

CONTENTS

Submitted for publication in 1980 by Nathalie Clerk,
Parks Canada, Ottawa.

PREFACE

Palladian-inspired architecture first became established and spread throughout England from 1710 to 1750. It was the first manifestation of a systematic interest in the basic precepts of classical architecture. This stage in the history of architecture was followed by the Neoclassical period (1750-1830), also oriented toward the expression of major classical principles. Unlike the Neoclassical architects, whose approach was based on the study of antiquity, their Palladian counterparts looked to the Italian Renaissance, and more particularly the works of Andrea Palladio (1508-80), for their inspiration.

This study examines the influence of the Palladian style on architecture in Canada from 1750 to 1830. Two other nineteenth century architectural style studies carried out by the Canadian Inventory of Historic Building are "The Neoclassical Style in Canadian Architecture" by Leslie Maitland, and "Domestic Architecture of the Picturesque in Canada: Villas and Cottages for Persons of Genteel Life and Moderate Fortune" by Janet Wright.

In preparing this study, we consulted the data of the Canadian Inventory of Historic Building. We considered many "classical" buildings constructed between 1750 and 1850, which for chronological reasons were located mainly in the Atlantic provinces, Quebec and Ontario, and from them we selected those with external features characteristic of the Palladian style, such as projecting frontispieces, pediments, lateral wings or Venetian windows.

We knew because of their age several of the buildings selected might have already disappeared by the time the Canadian Inventory of Historic Building collected its data. For this reason we also consulted various sources of iconographic archives, in particular at the Public Archives Canada (Ottawa), the Metropolitan Toronto Library (Toronto), the Archives nationales du Québec (Quebec City), the Musée du Québec (Quebec City), the Public Archives of Nova Scotia (Halifax), Dalhousie University (Halifax), the Museum of New Brunswick (Saint John), and the Provincial Archives of New Brunswick (Fredericton). We thus completed our selection and retraced

several buildings representative of the style but no longer standing.

We completed this selection of buildings by consulting primary and secondary sources, from which we obtained additional illustrations and historical information.

We then grouped the buildings selected according to their function: religious, public or domestic. This method of grouping revealed that the influence of the Palladian style was more direct and obvious on buildings of an official nature. It also showed that regional influences were particularly strong in the case of religious and domestic architecture, while public architecture was generally of a more uniform nature throughout the country. Thus the former two categories offered several representative examples of the Palladian style but featured mainly many regional adaptations. Often the Palladian influence was noted on vernacular-type buildings, or on buildings in the British classical tradition. Public architecture, however, was generally more homogeneous, partly, no doubt, because of its official nature, but also because of the various controls over design and construction exercised by the government of the day.

This method of grouping also revealed that certain regions offer few examples of the various types of Palladian buildings. There are several reasons for this uneven geographic distribution. One is of a chronological nature: obviously, the older regions are more likely to have produced Palladian buildings. We were unable to identify a single building of this style west of Ontario. It is also possible that some such buildings were destroyed or modified over the years, or that certain regions simply did not adopt this style, as in Newfoundland and Prince Edward Island where few examples are found, and in Ontario where few Palladian churches were constructed.

A collection of slides showing Canadian Palladian buildings is currently being prepared in collaboration with the National Film Board.

We thank Christina Cameron for her invaluable advice and comments throughout the course of this project. We also thank the following persons who in various ways assisted us in our research: Nicole Cloutier, Marc

Lebel, Leslie Maitland, A.J.H. Richardson, Janet Wright, and André Lamalice for his editing. Finally, we thank all the individuals and organizations who contributed either directly or indirectly to the preparation of this report, in particular the staff of the Public Archives Canada and the Canadian Inventory of Historic Building.

INTRODUCTION

This is a study of the influence of the Palladian style on Canadian architecture from 1750 to 1830. It defines the Palladian style in the context of eighteenth century England, determines how and why this style appeared and flourished in Canada, and finally identifies the buildings most representative of it.

Palladianism had its most direct and constant influence on our architecture from 1750 to 1830. However, it continued to be influential even after 1830, in both vernacular and official architecture, for some of its major principles remained in favour in the Neoclassical period. Indeed, some of its decorative elements were to remain popular until the end of the nineteenth century, particularly in vernacular architecture. Finally, certain stylistic currents of the late nineteenth century, such as the Georgian Revival, shingle style and Queen Anne style, were to incorporate certain elements of the Palladian vocabulary (in particular the Venetian window).

When was the term "Palladian" first applied to this architectural style? We know that English travellers visiting Canada at the beginning of the nineteenth century described this style of building as "modern,"[1] "English"[2] or "Anglo-American."[3] Sometimes they specified the architectural order used (such as the Doric order), but they never used the term "Palladian." Apparently it was in 1838, in England, that the word was first used in a stylistic context.[4] Although it was used to describe a building in Toronto in 1857,[5] it did not become general usage until the 1870s, when there began to be an interest in the architectural styles of the preceding century.

More recently, several authors, including John Summerson[6] and Rudolf Wittkower,[7] have questioned the use of this term, arguing that the Palladian style represented only a partial return to the work of the sixteenth century Italian architect Andrea Palladio. Rudolf Wittkower in particular persuasively argues that the Palladian architects were selective in their choice of Palladio's works and that they interpreted his techniques in light of their own architectural background and their needs. Furthermore, other, sometimes contradictory influences, including those

of Inigo Jones, Christopher Wren, Vitruvius and Scamozzi, are reflected in this style.

Although it is thus not entirely accurate, the term "Palladian" is nevertheless used to describe the architectural style that flourished in England from 1710 to 1750. It characterizes the dominant influence of this period. In the Canadian context, it is used to describe the influence of this style on the architecture of the English colonies after 1750.

A second term is also commonly used to describe the architecture of 1750-1830: "Georgian" is used to describe a building type that is classical in spirit and derives from the British architectural tradition. This building type, peculiar to England during the Georgian period, was introduced to the English colonies during the eighteenth century.

Apparently it was in "Georgian Houses of New England," an article by R.S. Peabody published in the United States on October 20, 1877, that this term was first used to describe a particular type of architecture.[8] The author, reflecting an interest that had existed since the 1850s,[9] advocated a return to the architecture of the colonial period, which he described as being natural and lacking any specific stylistic reference: "...From no field can suggestion be drawn by an artist more charming and more fitted to our usages, than from the Georgian mansions of New England."[10] Several of these houses offered "a classical detail universally used, the common language of every carpenter, and treated freely with regard only to comfort, cosiness, or stateliness, and with no superstitious preference for Palladio or Scamozzi."[11] His use of the word "Georgian," then, referred to a vernacular and functional architecture that reflected the great classical tradition. Later, the term was adopted by both American and Canadian authors, including Harold Donalson Eberlein,[12] Marcus Whiffen,[13] William H. Pierson, Jr.,[14] Eric Arthur,[15] Ramsay Traquair,[16] and Marion MacRae,[17] who used it with occasional attempts to qualify its meaning.

In fact, the term "Georgian" is used primarily to describe a historical period corresponding to the reigns of the four Georges who ruled England from 1714 to 1830. This long period saw the passage of various architectural styles, including Palladianism, Neoclassicism, the Picturesque, and Gothic Revival. It is therefore inaccurate to speak of a "Georgian" style. In the Canadian context, it is ambiguous to speak of "Georgian" architecture, because the term tends to confuse a type of building with a period of English history. In our opinion, it is preferable to speak of British classicism in describing a building style of British and classical origin, peculiar to England during the Georgian period, that was introduced in this country during the eighteenth century and that underwent numerous adaptations in Canada.[18]

Two terms are used frequently throughout this report: "Palladianism," to describe the specific influence of this style, and "British classicism," to describe a style of building derived from the great classical tradition emanating from England.

THE PALLADIAN MOVEMENT IN ENGLAND

Several authors have studied this period of English architectural history and have analysed the works of Andrea Palladio and his influence on eighteenth century architects. This section is an overview of the major principles and achievements of the Palladian Movement in England. It draws heavily on John Summerson's study on the origins and evolution of the movement in England;[1] Rudolf Wittkower's study on Palladio, Palladianism and the writings generated by the movement;[2] and James S. Ackerman's study on Palladio.[3]

Palladio

Palladio's great treatise, the celebrated *Quattro Libri dell'Architettura (The Four Books of Architecture)*, which was to have such a profound influence on an entire generation of architects, was published in Venice in 1570.[4] Its immediate success, both in Italy and abroad, was probably due to the fact that for the first time, the ideas of Vitruvius and Alberti were clearly explained. Other than Vitruvius's *De Architectura*[5] and Alberti's *De Re Aedificatoria*,[6] Palladio's main sources were the ruins of ancient Rome.[7]

His treatise is divided into four volumes. The first presents a system of architectural orders based on the module, along with commentaries on the various components of buildings; the second volume examines various public and private buildings located mainly in Venice and Vicenza; the third is devoted to bridges and streets; and the fourth volume examines temples.

Several of the most important rules presented by Palladio are contained in the first volume of his treatise. These rules emphasize the importance of the proportions of each part of a building and the need to achieve harmony between these various parts. It was precisely these rules that the Palladians adopted at the beginning of the eighteenth century.

At the beginning of the first volume, Palladio affirms the three goals of architecture as stated by Vitruvius — utility, durability and beauty — and lists various ways of attaining harmony between the various parts of a building and the whole. He suggests that the foundations be solidly built, that columns and openings be well placed to achieve a balance between spaces and volumes, and that the most massive columns be placed at the lower level of the building and spaced proportionately so that the entrance is emphasized.

To facilitate the execution of these recommendations, he establishes a unit of measurement that determines the dimensions of the columns and pilasters as well as the space separating them. This unit of measurement, borrowed from Vitruvius, is called the module, defined as the diameter of the column divided into sixty parts or minutes (except for the Doric column, where the module is given as half the diameter of the column divided into sixty minutes). Thus it is possible to express the proportions of the various parts of the orders.

In addition to this system of orders, the first volume includes a section in which Palladio denounces certain abuses. He condemns columns without bases, cartouches projecting from cornices, and cornices and other ornaments out of proportion with the building. The error he considers the most serious is the use of broken pediments. Created by the ancients as a protection against the rain, the pediment must, he argues, retain its whole upper part in order not to deviate from its primary function, which is above all utilitarian.

At the end of this first volume, Palladio explains how to establish the dimensions of the doors and windows. The windows on the ground floor should have identical dimensions, and those on each additional floor should decrease in height by one-sixth. He recommends that windows be located at some distance from the ends of a building and that those on either side of the facade be made to correspond.

Finally, Palladio suggests in the second volume of his treatise that rooms such as the kitchen, the cellar and the servants' quarters be located in the basement, and that the main rooms, such as the library and the entrance hall, be located on the main floor. He also recommends the hall be located in the central axis of the building and the rooms be arranged in symmetrical fashion.

Palladio's contribution is significant because he expressed clearly certain ideas that had been circulating in Italy since the fifteenth century, and he put into practice concepts that had until then remained theoretical. Among these were the harmony of proportions and especially the symmetry of the floor plan of the ground floor, advocated by various Renaissance architects. It is not difficult to imagine the interest Palladio's treatise held for early eighteenth century English architects, who were anxious to replace the Baroque principles of the preceding century. Palladio offered them a well-articulated vocabulary derived from the study of Vitruvius and Alberti and an analysis of the Roman ruins based on precise rules which were relatively easy to assimilate.

Origins of the Movement

Even though fifteenth and sixteenth century Italian architecture, particularly that of Palladio, did not become influential in England until the early eighteenth century, the country had been familiar with some of the ideas of the Renaissance since the beginning of the preceding century.

For example, the English architect Inigo Jones is known to have travelled in Italy in 1601 and 1613-14.[8] There he discovered the works of Palladio and measured and sketched the ancient monuments of Rome. On his return, he built the Queen's House (1616-35) at Greenwich, possibly the first English building illustrating the classical precepts of the Renaissance (Fig. 1). The building was innovative in that it introduced the concept of an isolated horizontal block which was defined in terms of the ratios between its various dimensions. But for a variety of political, social and economic reasons, the ideas advanced by Inigo Jones were not widely disseminated at the time.[9]

With the accession of George I to the throne in 1714, economic conditions developed under Charles II began to improve, and this, along with a certain political and social stabil-

ity, favoured the birth of a classical style that had been in gestation for some time.[10] The new Whig aristocracy, reacting against the tastes that had held sway in the Court for fifty years, showed itself to be highly favourable to a theory that called for a return to the Renaissance and suggested the development of a national style. The Palladian Movement enabled the new political elite to cast aside the Baroque style, which was associated with the preceding reign, and to create a new architecture based on rigorous laws. Finally, the arrival of these new ideas coincided with a boom in the construction of country houses.

The Palladian Movement was officially launched in 1715 with the publication of *Vitruvius Britannicus* by Colen Campbell.[11] One of the original features of this book was its appeal to the British architects of the day to free themselves of the Baroque influence and create a new type of building inspired by the works of the Italian Renaissance in general and Palladio in particular. As models, Campbell cited 100 buildings, most of which had been designed by Inigo Jones, and they had an immediate influence on English architecture.[12]

In 1716, Giacomo Leoni's English translation of *Quattro Libri dell'Architettura* by Palladio confirmed the importance that was henceforth to be accorded to the Italian architect.[13] Leoni's work was the first attempt to translate Palladio's entire treatise into English. Despite the stylistic alterations Leoni made to the original plates,[14] the existence of a publication of such magnitude — in terms of both its size and its cost — reflects the interest aroused by the architectural principles and achievements of Palladio.

These two publications ushered in the Palladian era. They contained in substance the major themes that would subsequently be developed in the numerous publications engendered by the movement.

Two generations of architects were to contribute to the development of Palladianism. The first group consisted at the outset of those who initiated it, in particular Colen Campbell and Richard Boyle, third Earl of Burlington. It was Campbell who, through his writings, actually launched the movement. His buildings rapidly became prototypes which influenced much of domestic architecture in England (Figs 2, 3).

Burlington, for his part, drew from the same sources as Campbell. He visited Italy in 1719 to study the works of Palladio. Much more doctrinaire than Campbell, he immediately became the leader of the movement. He published designs and encouraged others in the design and construction of buildings. The architectural works of William Kent, Roger Morris, Henry Flitcroft, Isaac Ware and John Vardy are generally associated with this first group of Palladians. With the rise of the second group, particularly Robert Taylor, James Paine and John Carr, the Palladian doctrine became more strict, and it gave rise to an elaborate, formal style against which the architects of the second half of the eighteenth century were to react.

Publications

Ushered in by two publications, the Palladian period was characterized by the appearance of a vast number of architectural treatises. An unprecedented number appeared between 1715 and 1750[15] and there were several reasons for this phenomenon. First, the period was marked by a surge in architecture-related activities; with greater interest in this field, there was a demand for specialized publications from which to draw models. Second, the economic, social and political climate was favourable to this type of publication. Finally, the dogmatic spirit of the Palladian Movement encouraged such works.

The mass of publications that appeared between 1715 and 1750 may be divided into four distinct groups: publications generated by Burlington; the writings of architects who, while following Burlington's line of thinking, were much more original in their approach; those of James Gibbs; and finally, the works of popularizers.

The publications of the first group gave new scope to the ideas of Palladio. They contributed to a better understanding of his works and those of Inigo Jones, while following the line of thought developed in *Vitruvius Britannicus*. Thus, under the direction of Burlington, architect William Kent in 1727 published the drawings of Inigo Jones;[16] the

following year architect Robert Castell published reconstructions of Roman houses and gardens in *Villas of the Ancients*; and finally, in 1738, architect Isaac Ware published a translation of Palladio's four-volume work.[17] Also noteworthy is *Fabbriche Antiche*, which Burlington himself published in 1730, and which reproduces drawings by Palladio of Roman baths.

The second group of publications was the work of authors who, although influenced by the ideas of Burlington, were notable for the originality of their approach. Thus an author named Ralph, whose identity is unclear, published in 1734 *A Critical Review of the Public Buildings, Statues and Ornaments in and about London and Westminster* in which, drawing on selected examples from these two cities, he severely criticized the state of English architecture. He condemned the Gothic style and advocated a strict Palladianism conforming to the models proposed by Burlington. Beyond this critical analysis, Ralph set out the major precepts of Palladian thought: that study and reflection are required for any architectural undertaking; that the architecture student must have a grounding in mathematics, geometry and design, as well as being endowed with genius, imagination and taste; and that these natural aptitudes must be accompanied by powers of observation.

What distinguishes Ralph's book from other publications of the period is that it was essentially theoretical. But the virulent tone that characterized this author's criticism of the architecture of his time was softened by several of his contemporaries.[18]

A second author in this group was Robert Morris. His six publications, which appeared from 1728 to 1757, dealt didactically with the major ideas of the movement. He outlined the basic rules to be followed in beginning the construction of a new building: find a suitable site, use high quality materials, and select competent workers.

He also formulated more precise rules regarding the composition of buildings. He insisted that each part of a building be complete in itself and thus contribute to the unity of the whole. He recommended use of the Greek orders rather than the Roman ones, which he considered to be less perfect. Finally, he proposed that rooms be laid out according to their importance, and that the external and internal parts of the building be proportional to each other; thus, a small building should have only small rooms.

Morris also provided advice on each part of the building. He explained that for the basement, rustic stones should be used to provide greater solidity. The ground floor should be separated from the basement by a plinth running around the building. The windows at ground level could be embellished with architraves and cornices. By contrast, the upstairs windows should be small and square, because this storey, used for sleep or study, required little light. Finally, Morris occasionally provided more technical instructions, on such matters as how to determine the proportions of a chimney or how to calculate the amount of light required in each room.

Morris was not as strict as Burlington; he permitted some departures from the rules established by the ancients: "...and though I may seem to have sometimes deviated from the Greek and Roman orders, yet where no established Rules can instruct, I have observed proportion."[19] He pointed out that Palladio himself had not rigorously applied the rules of the ancients, because he sometimes made concessions to Italian custom or the whims of the owner.

Contrary to the publications sponsored by Burlington, intended for an aristocratic readership, those of Morris were intended for well-to-do architecture enthusiasts or future clients. His precise and relatively simple explanations made Palladianism more accessible. Generally, the buildings he designed were country houses to be occupied by the middle class (Figs 7 and 8). For all these reasons, several of Morris's books were very popular in the American colonies.

The writings of James Gibbs constitute a third group of publications. Gibbs tended to be less dogmatic than the authors directly associated with Burlington's circle, and his models were even more accessible than those of Morris (Figs 9, 10 and 12). Probably because he was more practical than most other authors and because his plates were of better quality, his publications were immensely popular, both in England and in the colonies.

Some authors[20] assign Gibbs a particular place in the history of architecture, maintaining that he had affinities with both the

Baroque Movement and Palladianism. His approach was a highly personal one compared with that of Burlington's group, and he employed various techniques not found among the Palladians. His sources were also fairly diverse: Wren, Palladio, Jones and the Roman masters. Nevertheless, he did more to popularize the main principles of Palladianism than any other architect. Of course, Gibbs was not a dogmatic Palladian, but he cannot be dissociated completely from the movement.

The popularizers, whose publications constitute the fourth group, seldom distinguished between Palladio's works and those of Gibbs; rather, they drew their inspiration from both as from a single source. In the colonies, the popularity of Gibbs's writings — especially the *Book of Architecture* (1728) — did much to popularize Palladian principles and a certain Baroque tradition. Through his publications and his architectural models, Gibbs was too influential and, whether rightly or wrongly, is too closely associated with Palladianism to be completely disregarded in a study of this movement.

Whereas the other three groups of publications were generally intended for the aristocracy or the middle classes (as may readily be ascertained by examining the lists of subscribers to these publications), the popularizations tended to be addressed to the tradesmen (joiners and carpenters). Moreover, these books were written by such tradesmen rather than by architects. They represented a continuation of the tradition of books used by surveyors and mathematicians in the sixteenth and seventeenth centuries. These books were usually pocket-size and inexpensive. They made no real distinctions between their various sources of inspiration. Thus, Palladio and Gibbs were presented as products of the same classical tradition. By the 1740s, some of these books had become highly eclectic. They began to confuse classical sources with Gothic or even Chinese architectural sources.

With the middle class, builders and tradesmen as their primary audience, the publications of William Halfpenny are typical of these popularizations. From *Magnum in Parvo; or the Marrow of Architecture (1728) to A New and Complete System of Architecture* (1749), Halfpenny provided those with no knowledge of architecture with practical and simple techniques for designing such building components as windows, columns and arches (Fig. 11).

These popularizations reached an entirely different social group than the costly, prestigious works published by Burlington's group. They presented in simple, accessible form principles that had often been put forward abstractly. Whereas the treatises of Campbell and Burlington offered their readers models unaccompanied by precise technical data, the popularizations tended to present sections or parts of buildings along with instructions for builders wishing to imitate Palladio or convey the spirit of the ancients. These works did much to spread the Palladian vocabulary beyond the large urban centres. They had great influence in the colonies.

Thus, the principles of Palladianism were spread by two separate types of writings: treatises and popularizations. The latter publications were inspired by official architectural models and sources but brought these down to a more modest scale. They offered techniques for building according to the established principles. The treatises of Gibbs and Morris, in this context, occupied an intermediate position. Although inspired by the ideas of Burlington and his circle, they offered architectural models of greater simplicity and accessibility.

Buildings

Author John Summerson discerns two influential building types engendered by the Palladian Movement.[21] The first is what Summerson calls "House of Parade." Wanstead (1715-20), built in Essex by Colen Campbell, is an example (Fig. 2). It was, moreover, the first building in England to express so clearly the principles of classical Roman architecture. It was distinguished from buildings of Baroque inspiration by three major features: the horizontality of the facade, emphasized by the rusticated basement exterior and the arrangement of the openings and the cornice; the portico with six Corinthian columns supporting a pediment; and the absence of superfluous ornamentation. This design, consisting of a central block with a portico framed by lower lateral wings, remained popular until 1735. Campbell's Houghton Hall in Norfolk (1722)

is another example of the House of Parade. Again there is a central block with a portico, with the same horizontal divisions as Wanstead, but instead of lateral wings there are square towers. This type of composition was particularly popular during the 1740s and 1750s.

House of Parade was above all the expression of classical architectural principles. Architects of the eighteenth century remodelled the large late seventeenth century English houses according to a form made popular by Palladio.[22] The main elements they borrowed from Palladio were the functional difference between the basement, with its rusticated exterior, and the main floor (the *piano nobile*); an economy of detail, and a definite separation between the various parts of the building, as illustrated in certain of his palazzos and public buildings (Fig. 4).[23] The lateral wings, which in some cases frame the central block in House of Parade structures, were possibly inspired by some of Palladio's villas (Fig. 6).

The second type of building cited by Summerson is the villa.[24] In Palladio's time, the term "villa" referred to a large rural estate, including farm buildings and several houses. The main house on the estate was the *casa di villa*. In the eighteenth century, the term no longer designated a rural estate but merely a country house. For their villas, the Palladians imitated compact villas such as the Villa Rotonda (Fig. 5).

Compared with the House of Parade structure, the English villa was square and compact. It had a raised basement and, on each of its sides, a central pediment supported by columns.[25] Mereworth (1723) in Kent, by Colen Campbell, is a representative example (Fig. 3). Wanstead, Houghton Hall and Mereworth are usually considered prototypes of the English Palladian style, but a second generation of buildings was to combine the main characteristics of the two types.

When these elaborate buildings were being constructed, other architects such as James Gibbs and Robert Morris were proposing houses which, although more modest, were nevertheless also inspired by the main Palladian principles (Figs 7-10). Again, there was a facade organized horizontally, a raised basement, an accentuated *piano nobile* and a central portico. These buildings were more accessible than those of Campbell, Kent and

Burlington, and they popularized Palladian architecture among the middle class.

In short, whether in great residences or more modest houses, the Palladian style was easily identifiable in certain compositional features. Each part of the building was treated as an autonomous section and was linked to the whole in accordance with very strict symmetry. The most characteristic elements were concentrated in the central portion of the building. The facade of a Palladian building was divided into three horizontal parts: a raised basement with a rusticated exterior, a smooth-surfaced *piano nobile* with a central portico and rectangular windows sometimes embellished with pediments, and a smooth-surfaced upper storey with small, square windows lacking embellishment. The roof might be flat, with a cornice for adornment, or it might be hipped (particularly in the case of villas). The building sometimes had lateral wings extending out from the central block.

The interior layout consisted of a central hall surrounded by symmetrically placed rooms. Rooms such as the kitchen and servants' quarters were located in the basement; the major rooms (dining room, library and study) were located on the main floor, whereas bedrooms were generally upstairs.

Palladianism had a much less pronounced influence on urban architecture. As in country houses, the main floor of an urban house was sometimes given importance by the use of pilasters extending from the main floor to the roof. Alternatively, the presence of the orders might be merely implied — their imaginary presence might enter into the composition of the facade. However, the Palladian floor plan, with the principal rooms situated on the main floor, was not always easy to transpose to the urban setting. Nevertheless, a manner derived from Palladian models was gradually adopted there. Decorative elements, for their part, were incorporated in the facade much more freely.

Contrary to what occurred in domestic architecture, religious architecture exhibited different influences. The churches designed by Palladio were not very useful as models for eighteenth century architects. Palladio, using a device already adopted by Alberti and Bramante, masked the nave and aisles of the church with a central pediment flanked by two half pediments on the exterior, as at San Francesco della Vigna in Venice.

Instead, it was the models proposed by James Gibbs, particularly the Church of St. Martin-in-the-Fields (1721-26) in London, which influenced Anglican religious architecture during this period (Fig. 12). Gibb's immense popularity may be explained largely by the fact that his churches represented an advance over existing formulas (in terms of interior layout, organization of facades, and the position and form of the steeple), and that he used a simplified Palladian vocabulary. Also, his architectural models were accessible through his publications. He was the first author in his field — and indeed one of the few — to provide models of churches.

Public architecture during the Palladian period was almost nonexistent. Few public buildings were constructed during the reigns of George I and George II. Author John Summerson has identified two important public buildings: the Westminster Bridge and the Horse Guards building in London. The latter was designed by architect William Kent and constructed by J. Vardy in 1751-58. While Summerson acknowledges it was the most important building designed by the Burlington group, he is not sparing in his criticism of this structure. He writes that it shows the limits of Palladianism "and the unhappy results of trying to fit every contemporary problem into garments copied from the gear of a 16th century Italian."[26] The composition of this building is characterized by an excessive organization of its masses, which has the effect of undermining the unity of the whole.

During this period, then, most architectural activity was focussed on constructing houses, and most of the buildings proposed as models in the treatises were houses. Colonial builders wishing to construct public buildings therefore had to work from these domestic models.

INTRODUCTION OF THE PALLADIAN STYLE INTO THE COLONY

The form of Palladianism found in the colony, in both official and vernacular architecture, represents an interpretation and an often rather free adaptation of the style created in England. Various factors explain this situation, including several particularly evident in the subsequent analysis of buildings.

There were, firstly, factors inherent in the colony, including the quality of the materials available, the climate, and the training of the workmen, that necessitated changes in the proportions and layout which had characterized the great Palladian buildings. At the same time, because of a lack of capital, it was often necessary to simplify the design of the building. In addition, already established architectural traditions, particularly in Quebec, along with the traditions that certain groups of immigrants brought with them, also served to dilute the influence of this style.

To gain a clear understanding of the nature of the Palladianism that developed in Canada, it is useful to know how this style was transmitted and disseminated within the colony. Apparently four means of dissemination played a particularly significant role: the importation of new books, the contribution of the military, the contribution of immigrant groups, and the influence of an architect named François Baillairgé and a teacher named Jérôme Demers.

Books

Several of the publications of the Palladian Movement were imported to the colony, and this favoured the dissemination of the major principles and the main decorative motifs of this style. From 1750 to 1830 it is in the official architecture that the influence of these books is the easiest to identify, and probably the most genuine. Indeed, administrative correspondence and official documents indicate that on several occasions books on architecture were consulted in the course of designing and constructing certain buildings.

Thus as early as 1750, Governor Edward Cornwallis wrote that Marybone Chapel, constructed by James Gibbs in 1721-22, served as a model for St. Paul's Anglican Church in Halifax (Fig. 14), the first Anglican church in the country.[1] Thus apparently by this time some of Gibbs's architectural models were already known in the colony. It is even possible that the *Book of Architecture* (in which the plan and elevations of the chapel are reproduced) was already accessible.

Major William Robe, in a highly enlightening document, reveals the sources and models used in developing the plans for Holy Trinity Anglican Cathedral in Quebec City (1800-1804).[2] In particular, he mentions the names of Palladio (for the Ionic pilasters, the proportions of the main columns and their entablature), Alberti (for the pillars of the galleries), Vitruvius as interpreted by Vignola (for the Ionic window on the east side), and Blondel (for the capitals on the base of the organ) (Fig. 22). Similarly, in 1799, Jonathan Sewell mentions having consulted architectural treatises in designing the court house in Quebec City (Fig. 30).[3]

These few examples are clear evidence that builders sought models and did not hesitate to consult architectural treatises. At a time when architectural training was rudimentary, these works served as guides and reference books.

The arrival and establishment of a new society of English origin was to favour fairly early the importation of new architectural treatises. A brief survey of the contents of various libraries located in Quebec City in the late eighteenth and early nineteenth centuries revealed that books of English origin were beginning to circulate by the 1780s. Thus the 1785 catalogue[4] of the Quebec City public library (founded in 1779) lists not only Blondel's *Cours d'architecture* (1771 edition) but also Andrea Palladio's four-volume work (most probably Isaac Ware's 1738 edition).[5] In addition, the *Gazette de Québec* of September 6, 1787[6] announced the arrival of a shipment of books, including four works on architecture: *Skaife's Architecture, Everyman a complete builder, Carpenter's Guide,* and *The manner to secure Buildings from fire.*

As well as these new works, books by

French authors or authors particularly popular in France were also available.[7] Indeed, the works of Blondel, Vignole and Philibert de l'Orme were to continue to circulate in Quebec during much of the nineteenth century, as may be ascertained from the inventory of the belongings of François Baillairgé (1808),[8] the will of Thomas Baillairgé (1848),[9] and the architecture course prepared by Jérôme Demers (1828). In the late eighteenth century, books by authors popular in France were to be found side by side with those of other authors of English origin. This reflects fairly accurately the situation of architecture in Quebec, where the influence of French architecture was to remain strong throughout part of the nineteenth century, despite the fact that new models of English architecture became influential in the late eighteenth century.

Military Architects

A second factor explaining the development of Palladianism in the colonies is the architectural contribution of certain officers in the Corps of Engineers and the Artillery. Among their duties, the Royal Engineers were responsible for constructing certain civil and military buildings. On occasion, officers of the Artillery also helped in the design of certain buildings (thus, two officers of the Artillery, Major William Robe and Captain William Hall, prepared the plans for Holy Trinity Cathedral in Quebec City).

Some of these officer-designed buildings were strictly functional and bore no relationship to any specific architectural style, for example the barracks at Quebec City and Halifax. Others showed the rather conservative influence of British classicism, such as the Commissariat Building in St. John's, Newfoundland (1818-21), designed by Lieutenant Richard Vicars, a Royal Engineer. But still others particularly served to disseminate the Palladian style and some of the methods associated with it: Holy Trinity Anglican Cathedral is a fine example of the latter.

The architectural contribution of the officers of the Corps of Royal Engineers and the Artillery is particularly interesting because at the time, their training did not actually prepare them to perform the functions of an architect.[10] From 1746, the year in which the Royal Military Academy at Woolwich, England, was founded, until 1812, the year in which the education of the Royal Engineers was reformed, cadets destined for either the Artillery or the Corps of Engineers received the same training: their courses were mainly oriented toward arithmetic and military theory, as well as mathematics and its applications in the artillery and engineering. The cadet received only a few fairly rudimentary notions of architecture: he learned about perspective in the course on design,[11] and about the means of preparing plans, elevations and sections of buildings in fortified towns in the course on fortification and artillery.[12] It is noteworthy, however, that beginning in 1797, students had to copy a series of questions and answers relating to architecture, as well as architectural designs.[13] And beginning in 1808, in the course on fortification, the cadets learned the various parts of columns and entablatures and had to be able to sketch the different orders.[14] Thus various factors other than training were responsible for the military's architectural contribution, including the talent and interest certain individuals showed in this discipline, the practice of consulting books on architecture (a popular pastime during this period) and travels in other colonies (particularly in the case of the Royal Engineers).

Immigration

Another factor contributing to the rapid dissemination of Palladianism was the arrival of English officials in the country, including administrators and members of the clergy, who brought with them a knowledge of refined architecture of fairly recent origin. Their influence was to be particularly evident in the construction of official residences and public and religious buildings. They frequently drew on the main models of English architecture (as set forth in the treatises), or they attempted to imitate familiar buildings such as the family home or the parish church.

The Scottish, English and Loyalist immigrants also began, at the end of the eighteenth century, to influence the architecture of the colony. Their influence mainly took the form of new construction techniques (such as ways to work with wood and stone). They also introduced new architectural models, which tended to be either those of classical British architecture or vernacular interpretations of it. However, several decorative elements (Venetian windows, pediment and door framed by pilasters) were borrowed from the Palladian style. The contribution of these new arrivals in disseminating and adapting elements of the Palladian style was to be particularly important in domestic architecture.

François Baillairgé and Jérôme Demers

The final factor we identified as contributing to the dissemination of the Palladian style was peculiar to Quebec. It is of fundamental importance in understanding Quebec architecture from 1750 to 1830. It consists of the teachings of Abbé Jérôme Demers and the influence of François Baillairgé on Demers and on the development of architecture in Quebec.

The writings and influence of Abbé Demers have already been studied by various authorities, including Msgr Olivier Maurault,[15] Gérard Morisset[16] and Luc Noppen.[17] Apparently from 1800 to 1840, Jérôme Demers taught a succession of subjects at the Séminaire de Québec: first philosophy, then physics and astronomy, and finally architecture. It was the scarcity of books on architecture that prompted him to prepare courses in the latter subject. It was thus in 1828 that he completed his celebrated *Précis d'architecture*. This work was the first architectural treatise produced in the colony. It took up ideas that had already been in circulation in the Quebec City area, and that Demers had probably been teaching for the past several years, especially since François Baillairgé's return from Paris.

Baillairgé's stay in Paris (1778-81) had a major bearing on the development of architecture in Quebec. Even though Baillairgé did not actually study architecture in the French capital, he became aware of the rules governing this discipline, as may be seen in the annotations that he made in an architectural book in

his collection.[18] His interest in new architectural trends was demonstrated when, on his return, he became inspired by Palladian elements, particularly those in evidence in the Anglican cathedral at Quebec City, and integrated them into new or existing buildings. In this manner, Baillairgé helped to disseminate official Palladianism and paved the way for his son Thomas to discover the Neoclassical style.

It seems likely that François Baillairgé contributed to some of the ideas expressed in Demers's *Précis*. For example, Demers attached great importance to theoretical and practical concepts from fields related to architecture, and to knowledge of the orders and the ratios associated with each. His description of the training required by an architect corresponds fairly closely to that received by François Baillairgé thirty years earlier.[19] The influence of Baillairgé and his son Thomas on Demers is also evident where the latter makes reference to their work methods.

The main sources of Jérôme Demers's *Précis* were the publications of Philibert de l'Orme, Vignole, d'Aviler and Jean-François Blondel. François Baillairgé likely discovered these authors while in Paris. He is known to have owned a book on architecture by Vignole. These authors could at that time be consulted at the library of the Séminaire de Québec and at the Quebec City public library.

Where, then, does Demers stand in relation to Palladianism? His *Précis* makes only one reference to Gibbs. This is in a commentary in which Demers criticizes the location of the galleries in certain Anglican churches.

> In the Anglican churches, built according to the designs of Mr. James Gibbs, the famous English architect, it is not uncommon to put galleries one-third or halfway up the shaft of the column; this is a serious error, since the column, by its nature, should always be isolated, and is not high enough to support horizontal burdens.[20]

In the origin and diversity of his sources, Demers reflects classical French thought as taught under Louis XVI, with which François Baillairgé might have come into contact in Paris at the end of the eighteenth century. The French school is known to have been much less selective than the English school. From its founding in 1671, the Académie royale d'architecture attributed considerable importance not only to the orders and proportions of Palladio, but to the Renaissance as a whole. Its interest in Scamozzi, Serlio and Alberti was fully as great as its interest in the illustrious Palladio. Demers's *Précis*, then, transmitted a concept of French architecture in which Palladio's influence was blended with that of several other masters. It introduced new ideas and architectural models derived from those of the Académie royale d'architecture, which would subsequently be the basis for the works of Thomas Baillairgé.

Each in his own way, François Baillairgé and Jérôme Demers helped to create an atmosphere receptive to the introduction of a new stylistic current. Baillairgé, through his architectural works, established a transition from the art of the French regime to that of the 1830s, and he introduced Palladian elements into the traditional architecture of Quebec. For his part, Jérôme Demers disseminated the new ideas in a more theoretical fashion, without necessarily promoting Palladianism. Because of these contributions Baillairgé and Demers are important figures in the architectural history of Quebec and in the development of a form of Palladianism adapted to Quebec.

RELIGIOUS ARCHITECTURE

Certain churches built by James Gibbs, as well as several of his designs which were published although never implemented, exerted a profound influence on English religious architecture in the eighteenth century. Soon St. Martin-in-the-Fields in London became a prototype for Anglican churches everywhere — not only in England but also in the colonies (Fig. 12). This success may be explained by the fact that colonial builders modelling their churches on St. Martin-in-the-Fields could easily make changes according to the availability of materials and the experience of the workmen, at the same time maintaining an architectural manner reminiscent of the home country.

In the United States, the first manifestations of Gibbs's influence date from the mid-eighteenth century. Several authors, including William H. Pierson, Jr.[1] and Harold Donaldson Eberlein,[2] have studied Gibbs's influence on American religious architecture. Their studies have shown that this influence was most obvious in the organization and ornamentation of the facade, as well as in the arrangement and type of openings (Christ Church in Philadelphia, Pennsylvania, 1727-54), the position and type of steeple (St. Michael's Church in Charleston, South Carolina 1752-61), and lastly the layout of the interior of the church (First Baptist Meeting House in Providence, Rhode Island, 1774-75) (Fig. 20).

In Canada, Gibbs's influence on religious architecture is often reflected in the same manner, and also dates from the mid-eighteenth century. It first emerged in certain large centres, subsequently spread to outlying areas, and finally reached the more remote communities, in some cases fairly late in the nineteenth century. The greatest number of churches influenced by Palladianism are in Quebec and Nova Scotia. Churches in regions settled at the beginning of the nineteenth century tend to be of the much more recent Neoclassical type. This is particularly true in the case of what is now Ontario, where very few Palladian churches were built (Fig. 29).

There is a close relationship between the emergence of the Palladian style in Canada and the introduction of the Anglican faith. We know that the Church of England first established itself in the garrison towns (Halifax 1749-50, and Quebec City 1760), where it was assured of prestige and assistance by virtue of its relations with the government. The latter supported the construction of churches to clearly demonstrate that the Church of England was established on Canadian soil. It was only natural, in these circumstances, to turn to the established architectural models associated with this faith in England, namely those of Gibbs. For this reason, the first Anglican buildings in Halifax and Quebec City were those that resembled most closely the prototypes designed by Gibbs (Figs 14, 22). Builders of the more modest Anglican churches in small towns and remote areas, and of churches of other faiths, tended to adapt and simplify the more striking features of the large Anglican churches and often combined them with elements of architectural traditions associated with their own region.

The descriptions provided by travellers who visited the colony in the late eighteenth and early nineteenth centuries contain vital information on the appearance of these new houses of worship. These descriptions are useful in confirming the introduction of the new architectural models of English origin into the colony, as well as the interest that the style of some of these buildings aroused. It is noteworthy, however, that these travellers, who were mostly English, were necessarily more sensitive to a style of architecture that was already familiar — hence the laudatory comments often aroused by new Palladian-inspired churches and the lack of attention given to small, traditional churches. Finally, we found no description of a Palladian church in Upper Canada, supporting the theory that few Palladian churches were built in this region.

The Anglican cathedral in Quebec City (1800-1804) aroused the greatest number of travellers' comments (Fig. 22). John Lambert, for example, wrote in 1806-1808 that this building was modelled on St. Martin-in-the-Fields.[3] George Heriot wrote in 1807 that while it was not ornate, this building was elegant, "...the rules of architecture having been adhered to in its structure."[4] In 1818-19, Edward Allen Talbot also commented that the church had been built according to the rules of architecture.[5] There were numerous similar comments.

Christ Church Anglican Cathedral in Montreal (1805-20) also elicited favourable comment (Fig. 23). Talbot wrote in 1823 that it was one of the most attractive buildings in the city. He cited the elegance of the steeple, considered to be the finest of its kind in British North America.[6] The following year, Benjamin Silliman also commented on the beauty of this building.[7]

Churches in the Atlantic region aroused few travellers' comments; such comments as there were concerned the materials used and the form of the buildings. Thus Patrick Campbell commented that the outside of Trinity Anglican Church in Saint John, New Brunswick (1788-91), was so well painted that it might easily have been taken for a stone building (Fig. 17).[8] John McGregor in 1828[9] and E.T. Coke in 1832[10] both commented on the circular shape of St. George's Anglican Church in Halifax (1800-1801) (Fig. 21).

Atlantic Provinces

In 1750 the governor of Nova Scotia, Edward Cornwallis, wrote that the frame of St. Paul's Anglican Church in Halifax (Fig. 15) had been constructed in Boston modelled on James Gibbs's Marybone Chapel (Fig. 13).[11] The colonial authorities looked to New England for the construction of the frame of this building and to England for its design; thus for this first Anglican church in Canada, they turned to two external centres capable of offering quality services and models.

Governor Cornwallis's comments are evidence that certain architectural prototypes of Gibbs were known at this time in the English colonies. The plan and elevations of Marybone Chapel were published in the *Book of Architecture* (plates XXIV and XXV), so likely builders had access to Gibbs's model through this publication.

An engraving made by Richard Short in 1759 shows St. Paul's Church as it appeared before the various alterations it underwent during the nineteenth century (Fig. 14). At the time, it was a rectangular building, the south facade of which featured a large Venetian window framed by two round-headed windows and two doors. The design of this facade was indeed inspired by the one presented by Gibbs in his *Book of Architecture* (plate XXV) (Fig. 13). The steeple of the church in Halifax, consisting of two cupolas resting on a square base, was also very similar to the one on Marybone Chapel. The same arrangement was also used for the side windows, namely a double row of round-headed windows, with the lower ones being smaller. Certain departures from Gibbs's model, such as the reduction in the size of the pediments and columns, may have been dictated by the use of wood.

Because St. Paul's was to be the first Anglican church on Canadian soil, it was built with an attention to detail such that it compared favourably with certain parish churches in England and some of its contemporaries in New England. Most of the churches subsequently built elsewhere in Nova Scotia and New Brunswick were less elaborate.

St. Mary's Anglican Church, Auburn, Nova Scotia (1790), is representative of these small churches which adopted the new architectural vocabulary in modified form (Fig. 16). The angle of its pediment is less pronounced than on the monumental churches. At the same time, it exhibits considerable detail: the steeple and the round-headed windows are framed by pilasters, and the pilasters on either side of the main door are topped by capitals.

Trinity Anglican Church in Saint John, New Brunswick (1788-91), which is no longer standing, is another example of this type of church (Fig. 17). It was a fairly large, rectangular wooden structure. Its facade was embellished with wooden imitation pilasters, a pediment with a semicircular window, round-headed windows featuring keystones, and a portico. All these elements gave the building a certain monumental appearance. St. Andrew's Presbyterian Church in Saint John, New Brunswick (ca. 1814) was another church modelled on monumental antecedents (Fig. 18). It also illustrates the Palladian influence on the architecture of a non-Anglican church.

In addition to these churches that adopted several of the elements of monumental architecture, there were during this period several houses of worship entirely uninfluenced by Palladianism in their design. Many of these buildings were of the "meeting house" type, a Loyalist architectural tradition originating in England. Originally, the meeting house structure resembled a private dwelling, but gradually it evolved to accommodate a steeple in front and a sanctuary at the rear. The addition of the steeple shifted the entrance from the long side of the building to the short side. The differences between the meeting house and the traditional church began to blur early in the nineteenth century when Palladian elements were commonly being introduced.

Greenock Presbyterian Church in St. Andrews, New Brunswick (1821-24), illustrates this final stage in the evolution of the meeting house (Fig. 19). It is a two-storey, rectangular wooden structure, the sides of which feature the double row of rectangular windows found on numerous meeting houses. The front, with its steeple, is that of a church. The placement of the steeple at the front rather than on the peak of the roof is characteristic of the architecture of Christopher Wren.[12] At the same time, certain other elements of the building, such as the Venetian window, the round-headed window, the pediment on the steeple, and the pediments on the front and rear facades, denote the influence of Gibbs.

This building represents a perfect synthesis of the various influences in play in the Atlantic provinces: the influence of the Loyalists may be seen in the material used and the meeting house type of structure, while the influence of the British (Wren and Gibbs) is embodied in the steeple, pediments and openings. It is difficult not to compare this church with certain houses of worship in New England, such as the First Baptist Meeting House in Providence, Rhode Island (Fig. 20). The various similarities in the religious architecture of the Atlantic provinces and New England may be explained not only by the geographical proximity of these two regions, which favoured immigration to Canada and thus the dissemination of techniques and stylistic elements, but also by the use of the same material — wood — and the existence of common architectural models derived from England.

This examination of the Palladian influence in this region of the country is not complete without mention of St. George's Church in Halifax (1800-1801), particularly noteworthy for its circular design (Fig. 21). Owing to this design, it conforms more closely than any other Canadian church to one of Palladio's principles, according to which the circle is both technically and philosophically the most appropriate form for temples, being the simplest, strongest and most regular. From a technical standpoint, a circular building contains much more space than its four-sided counterpart, whereas from the philosophical standpoint, it illustrates divine justice, because it has neither beginning nor end and all its parts are identical.[13]

The English Palladian architects liked the circular form but used it only occasionally, particularly for summerhouses. Gibbs's initial plans (ca. 1721) for the church of St. Martin-in-the-Fields were for a circular structure. These plans were even reproduced in the *Book of Architecture* (plates VIII-XV).

St. George's is the only Canadian church of its time to have adopted this type of design. Some authors attribute its use to the Duke of Kent.[14] Two other buildings constructed under his auspices use the same form: the town clock in Halifax (Fig. 49) and the music pavilion at the Prince's Lodge, both designed by William Hughes.

Thus, two major influences left their mark on religious architecture in the Atlantic provinces from 1750-1830. First, the Loyalist influence from New England was evident in the use of wood construction techniques such as clapboard siding and in the introduction of the meeting house as a building type. Second, the English influence, whether through books or workmen, administrators or clergy coming to the region directly from England itself or via New England, took the form of new Palladian-inspired stylistic elements. This latter stylistic influence was first felt in the large centres (Halifax and Saint John), which were receptive to the appearance of monumental, refined architecture in the English tradition. It was also expressed in the architecture of more numerous but more modest buildings, which borrowed from Palladianism its most striking features, such as the front pediment, the Venetian window, the steeple and the portico. For such buildings, the Palladian style provided new decorative elements.

Quebec

To understand the influence of the Palladian style on religious architecture in Quebec, it is necessary to take a step backward in time. By the year 1760, Quebec already had an architectural tradition dating back more than a century. This tradition was based partly on French models transmitted by the ecclesiastical administration and the builders themselves. It was also the result of a gradual adaptation to local conditions, namely the climate, the nature of the building materials and the availability of manpower.

Throughout the French regime, the architecture found in the urban centres of Quebec City and Montreal resembled European models. Two churches, Notre-Dame in Montreal (1721-23) and Notre-Dame in Quebec City (1744-48), reconstructed by Gaspard Chaussegros de Léry, are representative of this monumental architecture derived from academic models and produced by French builders.

The influence of the great academic models, having been filtered through the urban colonial models, was more modest and less formal on churches in smaller parishes. These parish churches gradually adopted several standard plans: the "maillou" plan (nave with a semicircular apse) the Récollet plan (nave with a chancel), and the Jesuit plan (nave with transept).[15] Thus a religious architecture developed that by the mid-eighteenth century had become relatively remote from its French models, yet was admirably suited to the conditions that prevailed in the colony.[16]

What was the effect of the arrival of new models on this architecture? Until 1800, it was practically negligible mainly because the members of the Protestant communities, who were largely merchants or soldiers, until then numbered too few to undertake the construction of new churches. These communities had to make do with existing buildings. Thus the Anglican community in Quebec City used the chapel of the Récollets until it was destroyed in 1796, and did not acquire a new building until 1804. Similarly, the Presbyterian community in Quebec City gathered to worship at the college of the Jesuits until 1809. Following the circulation of a petition calling for a building large enough to accommodate an ever expanding community, construction began on St. Andrew's Church. In Montreal the Anglican community had to use first the chapel of the Ursulines, then the church of the Récollets until 1804, and finally St. Gabriel's Church until 1814, when Christ Church was completed.

At the beginning of the nineteenth century the Protestant communities expanded considerably, owing to an influx of Loyalists and English immigrants.[17] These communities began to exert pressure on the authorities to obtain new churches. It was also at this time that several English and Scottish immigrants trained in the construction trades arrived.[18] By participating in the construction of these new churches, they greatly assisted in introducing techniques and stylistic elements in use in England and New England.

As for the Francophone community, before 1800 it was confined to repairing or enlarging existing churches. An order issued on April 30, 1791 sanctioned construction and repair work on churches and presbyteries used under the French regime.[19] But it was not until the end of the second decade of the nineteenth century, following the construction of Anglican churches, that the Palladian style began to influence the traditional religious architecture of Quebec.

Holy Trinity Anglican Cathedral in Quebec City (1800-1804) (Fig. 22), erected by two officers of the Royal Artillery, was the first religious building constructed in Quebec to reflect the Palladian influence so directly, and it was designed as the most faithful Canadian imitation of the English model, St. Martin-in-the-Fields.

Major William Robe, who, with Captain William Hall, designed the building, wrote a most interesting account of the process in which he mentions the authors consulted.[20]

> The general dimensions of this Church were in great measure taken from those of the Church of St. Martin's, in the Fields, London, the state of materials and workmanship in Canada made a plain design necessary.
>
> The east and west ends are ornamented with pilasters of the Ionic according to Palladio and supporting a modillion cornice and pediment but without a frieze; this idea was taken from

the Pantheon at Rome so executed, and was done to give more boldness to the pilasters for the intended height of the building. The pilasters project less than Palladio's rule directs, owing to the Pointe-aux-Trembles stone, which, in the then state of the quarries could not be got in masses large enough without an enormous expense. The pediments are surmounted with oblate vases which at the angles of the buildings serve as flues for the stoves within the Church....

The proportions of the main columns and entablatures [on the interior] are from Palladio, as correctly followed as wood work would admit....

The galleries with the pillars under the organ are from Alberti's proportions, the volutes formed in his manner, and the only deviation from him is the dentel added to the cornice Alberti giving two plain faciae....

The east window is the Ionic of Vitruvius according to Vignola, the shafts having a small addition of length to suit the opening.

The pulpit is the Ionic of Alberti, the design of it and the reading desks are my own.

The pillars supporting the stairs behind the pulpit are taken from some peculiarly plain Pilars in the Coliseum at Rome. The organ is a design of my own and is yet incomplete, the base of the large case is moulded from the Ionic of Vitruvius, and the capitals intended for it are from an open network design in the temple of Erecthia at Athens and described in Blondel's works, now in the Québec Library. The temporary caps on the Choir organ are gilt with scroll ornaments from the same....[21]

Nevertheless, some of the elements of the facade of this cathedral, such as the pediment, the arcade and the steeple, were especially influential for religious architecture in the Quebec City area. They represented stylistic innovations that subsequently would be gradually incorporated into structures of more modest dimensions.

Christ Church Anglican Cathedral in Montreal, designed by William Berczy, is another example of Palladian architecture (Fig. 23). Its facade, featuring a Doric pediment supported by Tuscan pilasters, is divided into three sections, each containing a door, corresponding to the three interior divisions. Overall, the facade is designed to create the impression of monumentality, particularly evident when it is viewed at an angle. From this perspective, clearly the facade is much higher than the body of the building. The cornice running along its top adds to the impression by creating the illusion that the roof is flat, as at St. Martin-in-the-Fields. The steeple, constructed in 1819-20, apparently was derived from an idea of Gibbs for St. Martin's (*Book of Architecture*, plate XIX, 3rd proposal). While basically in the Palladian tradition, this church also has certain more recent Neoclassical features (recessed panels and volutes), inspired by buildings designed by the Adams brothers and common in England in the mid-eighteenth century. They were found here too, in religious and public architecture, particularly during the 1820s and 1830s.

These two churches are particularly refined examples of Palladian architecture, and both are evidence of a good understanding of the style. Furthermore, Major Robe's written account shows a knowledge of architecture and the great architects. Robe may have acquired some of this knowledge during his training, but likely he also consulted architectural treatises. William Berczy, however, probably studied architecture at the Academy of Vienna.[22] Holy Trinity Cathedral in Quebec City and Christ Church in Montreal were the first buildings constructed for the Anglican communities in these two cities. To signify the presence of this denomination in a prestigious manner, the authorities turned to Gibbs's architectural models, already associated with the mother church in England.

These two churches were to influence religious architecture in their respective areas, and this influence was to extend not only to other Anglican churches, but also to Catholic and Presbyterian ones, and to renovated buildings as well as new ones. In all cases, the elements borrowed from the Palladian style were largely decorative, a phenomenon explained by the persistence of construction techniques and architectural models carried over from the French regime. Especially striking features of Palladianism, such as the wide pediment, the Venetian window and the round-headed windows, were borrowed and incorporated into traditional structures. Also borrowed from Palladianism was the organization of the facade, particularly regarding the location of openings and the position of the steeple. These features gave the churches a new monumental aspect.[23]

The Palladian influence is evident in a group of parish churches constructed at the beginning of the nineteenth century. These buildings, of generally modest dimensions, combined a traditional plan with Palladian ornamentation. St. Stephen's Anglican Church in Chambly is a good example of this (Fig. 24). Its traditional plan consists of a rectangle opening onto a semicircular apse. The use of fieldstone, except for the portal, is a traditional construction technique. On the other hand, the apse is illuminated by a Venetian window, and the square-based steeple rests on the peak of the roof. Moreover, the facade is composed of a false pediment with returned eaves framing a fanlight, and the windows are embellished with keystones.

Similarly, St. Antoine Catholic Church in Longueuil (1810-13) combines a traditional plan by Abbé Conefroy with a Palladian facade (Fig. 25). Abbé Conefroy's plan, derived from a plan used under the French regime, provides for a nave cut by a transept, with a semicircular apse at the end.[24] The facade, however, denotes new influences. The pediment supported by a projecting section of the facade recalls the device of pilasters supporting the pediment on the Anglican cathedral in Quebec City, and on Montreal's Christ Church Cathedral, which was then under construction. An old engraving of the church of St. Antoine indicates that the facade was much higher than the body of the building, as was the case with Christ Church Cathedral.

The Palladian influence is also evident in the alterations made to older churches at the beginning of the nineteenth century, as may be seen in St. James Anglican Church in Trois-Rivières (Fig. 26). Constructed in 1754, this church was occupied by the Récollets until 1776.[25] Its very simple plan was fairly faithful to the "maillou" plan: it featured a rectangular body with round-headed windows along the sides (although the normally semicircular chevet was flat). After 1776, the church passed into the hands of the Anglican community, which in 1823 remodelled the building, changing mainly the roof, the interior layout and the steeple. Clearly these changes were intended to transform the former church of the Récollets into a traditional Anglican church.

St. Andrew's Presbyterian Church in Quebec City (1809-10) also illustrates this type of adaptation to the new architectural fashion (Fig. 27). The changes made to the building in 1823-24 are characteristic of Palladianism: the pediment, the steeple and the semicircular openings (since eliminated) above the doors.

A third building remodelled according to the tastes of the day was St. Gabriel's Presbyterian Church in Montreal, also known as Scotch Church (Fig. 28). Constructed in 1792, this church was remodelled in 1809 with a new roof, a steeple and a bell. Following these changes, the building offered a partial and rudimentary grouping of Palladian traits. Its facade featured a wide pediment, somewhat out of scale with the facade as a whole; light penetrated the pediment through an oculus; and the openings were ornamented with keystones and quoins, after the manner of Gibbs.

Similar alterations were made to Catholic churches. Between 1810 and 1820, the facades of several older churches were remodelled. Such a change generally affected the slope of the roof, the pediment and the steeple. Luc Noppen, in *Les églises du Québec*, cites several examples of this operation,[26] including François Baillairgé's 1816 remodelling of Notre-Dame-des-Victoires (1688). Baillairgé reduced the slope of the roof, applied a false pediment to the facade and put a small steeple on the roof. In 1818 Baillairgé also remodelled Quebec City's second Notre-Dame Cathedral (1766-71), adding a central pediment and extending the roof. Similarly, in Berthierville, Ste Geneviève Church (1782-87) was remodelled from 1816 to 1821, adding several Palladian features.

The influence of Palladianism on Quebec's traditional churches, then, was generally not extensive, because apparently existing architectural traditions, inherited from the French regime, were solidly established. The new architectural models appeared in the cities (Quebec City and Montreal), and their influence was felt mainly in neighbouring areas. Smaller, outlying parishes, however, tended to perpetuate the modes inherited from the old regime.

And in the large centres, just as in the smaller, outlying parishes, the plan, overall decorative treatment and interior layout of Catholic churches were not influenced by the Anglican models. Only the organization and ornamentation of the facade were borrowed from the Palladian style. The influence of the new style was primarily decorative. Only those stylistic elements that were most striking and also most adaptable to existing structures were copied. Thus Anglican churches located in the large centres offered the most refined examples of the new Palladian architecture, just as in the Atlantic region.

The period 1750-1830 saw the introduction and establishment of new models of religous architecture, particularly in the Atlantic region and in Quebec. The new style was introduced initially in the large centres, where the size of the Anglican community favoured the construction of churches characterized by a certain monumentality. These buildings were designed according to contemporary English models already associated with the Anglican church. When small churches were built or the facades of older ones remodelled, some elements of the new style were utilized.

St. Paul's in Halifax, Holy Trinity in Quebec City, and Christ Church in Montreal undoubtedly inspired an architectural trend among other churches. Also, the immigration of workmen from England and New England disseminated the new stylistic elements. But several churches constructed then bore little or no trace of the new architectural fashion, and for some, the Palladian influence remained essentially decorative.

The same phenomenon thus occurred in the two regions: the buildings most representative of the Palladian style appeared first, the churches built afterward adopted in modified form the layout and decoration of these first buildings. However, apparently the reasons for adopting the Palladian style varied according to denomination: the Anglican churches drew on Gibbs's models for reasons of faith and sometimes prestige, whereas the others did so essentially for decorative purposes.

PUBLIC ARCHITECTURE

Social and economic conditions in England during the Palladian period were favourable to the construction of great houses and villas.[1] Reflecting this emphasis on domestic architecture, the models presented in the architectural treatises were almost exclusively designs for houses and villas. Thus, when builders in the colonies constructed public buildings, they drew on models for domestic architecture, since these were the most accessible. Because of the size and often the complexity of the public buildings thus constructed, several resembled more closely the great domestic models proposed in the treatises than the majority of houses built in the colony.

Until the turn of the nineteenth century, the colony made do with temporary structures, but then buildings were built whose dimensions and character were better suited to the colony's needs. This group of public buildings (prisons, court houses, official residences, etc.), constructed between 1799 and approximately 1830, was especially influenced by the Palladian style.

Unlike religious or domestic architecture, Palladian-inspired public architecture had no obvious regional characteristics and presented a certain homogeneity. There were various reasons for this. The generalized use of a single building material — stone — partially accounted for this homogeneous character, along with the fact that a single colonial government was responsible for the construction of several of these buildings. Because such buildings were designed by people with the same training and same knowledge of English architecture, they were less likely to feature regional adaptations.

Lastly, various constraints peculiar to the colony account for the uniformity of these buildings as well as their often conservative character compared with what was being built at the same time in England. Because of monetary constraints, it was sometimes necessary to reduce dimensions and limit ornamentation; and it was often the elements considered most fashionable in England that were thus sacrificed. The availability or lack of certain materials, the level of experience of the workmen on hand, and finally the climate were other factors that could affect the size of the buildings or the amount of ornamentation incorporated in them.

Did travellers of the day react to this public architecture? Generally they showed little enthusiasm for it until nearly 1820. They commented mainly on its bare, functional appearance. This, for example, is what George Heriot wrote about public architecture in Quebec City in 1807:

> In most of the public buildings, no great degree of taste or elegance can be discovered, although much labour and expense must have been bestowed on their construction. The architects seem principally to have had in view, strength, and durability, and not to have paid much regard to these rules of their art which combine symmetry with utility.[2]

In 1818 John Palmer expressed the same opinion regarding the public buildings in Montreal and Quebec City, describing them as mainly functional and inelegant.[3] According to Edward Allen Talbot in 1818–19, Quebec City's public buildings aroused little interest in anyone used to seeing magnificent architecture in the cities of Europe; he added, however, that buildings recently constructed in Montreal were of better quality.[4] Two buildings in Quebec City were the object of somewhat more attention and comment during this period: the court house and the Château Saint-Louis.[5] During his stay in this city in 1816-17, Lieutenant Francis Hall wrote that the facade of the Château Saint-Louis "resembles that of a respectable gentleman's house in England."[6] Two years later, Benjamin Silliman wrote that the court house in Quebec City was "a modern stone building...with a handsome and regular front" (Fig. 30).[7]

But certain buildings located in the Atlantic region, particularly in Halifax, elicited the most laudatory comments. Mainly noted were Dalhousie College[8] and Province House in Halifax, and Government House in Fredericton. Haliburton wrote in 1823 that Province House in Halifax was not only the best constructed but also the most handsome legislative building in North America (Fig. 35).[9] According to E.T. Coke in 1832, the official residence in Fredericton surpassed the ones in Quebec City and York in terms of both siting and architectural style (Fig. 37).[10]

In short, these travellers, most of whom were of British origin, were naturally responsive to an architecture that reminded them of familiar models. They were especially inclined to remark on certain monumental buildings such as official residences and legislative buildings. They noted few public buildings in Upper Canada. Indeed, our survey revealed very few public buildings constructed in Upper Canada during this period, and apparently this region adopted Neoclassical architectural models earlier than the rest of Canada.

Buildings from 1750 to 1830 showing the influence of Palladianism may be classified into five groups. The first group is characterized by a rectangular plan with a projecting frontispiece in front, as popularized by Gibbs (Figs 9, 10). This is the design that became most popular. It appeared in 1799 and was used until the later 1830s. The importance of the ornamentation on these buildings varied over the years. The period from 1799 to 1815 was one of sobriety, with very few decorative elements. The central part of the facade was emphasized by a simple projecting section surmounted by a pediment. Then from 1815 to 1830, the building treatment became more complex, and the decoration more diverse. In some cases, the central part was even emphasized by pilasters or columns supporting a pediment.

Most of the buildings corresponding to the first stage of the development of this formula were located in Quebec, and generally they were prisons and court houses. The Quebec City court house (1799-1803) is one of the first buildings to have a projecting frontispiece in its central portion (Fig. 30). The Montreal court house is another version of this building type (Fig. 31). Its decoration was much more extensive: a cornice ornamented with modillions, a pediment decorated with an emblem and surmounted by an urn, arcades surrounding the windows of the projecting part, and Venetian windows in the outward-projecting lateral wings.

Such wings projecting outward from either end of the facade of a building were an unusual feature for buildings in the colony. They were to be seen on several English Palladian buildings such as Colen Campbell's Houghton Hall (1722) and William Kent's Holkam Hall (1734), and in these cases the lateral sections dominated the rest of the facade. It was mainly Gibbs who designed buildings with projecting side sections that were truly integrated into the facade, as may be seen in his elevation of a house "for a person of quality" in Somersetshire (*Book of Architecture*, plate XXXVII) and his elevation of a house in Northamptonshire (plate XXXVIII).

The old Montreal prison (1808-1809) also featured a projecting front section (Fig. 32). The building's only decorative elements were the stone stringcourse demarcating the two storeys, the quoins and the cupola. The Trois-Rivières prison (1816-19), designed by François Baillairgé, used the same formula, but the presence of a third storey gave it an imposing appearance (Fig. 33).

These buildings, constructed at the beginning of the nineteenth century, had in common the composition of their facade, derived from that of the great houses built in England a century earlier. Their decoration consisted of elements popularized by Gibbs: quoins, cupolas, courses, emblems, rusticated stone. These embellishments, however, were subdued compared with those applied to buildings constructed after 1815, particularly in the Atlantic region. In terms of both their use of an English model and their simple ornamentation, this group of buildings represented a well-defined period in the development of public architecture. Both in their dimensions and in their stone construction, they expressed a desire for permanence. Borrowing features from a style originating in England, although sometimes austerely presented, was a new architectural development which heralded the more complex buildings of later years.

The Quebec prison (now Morrin College) (1808-11), designed by François Baillairgé, belongs within this first group of buildings but is distinguished from it by a calculated use of the architectural formula featuring a frontispiece (Fig. 34). The building consists of a rectangular block with a frontispiece projecting considerably from the building. Whereas such structures were usually integrated fairly harmoniously with the rest of the building, this one is dramatically emphasized, owing to its dimensions and ornamentation. In designing this building, Baillairgé borrowed an architectural formula from Philibert de l'Orme.[11] However, the commissioners responsible for overseeing the construction obliged Baillairgé to omit the cornice and pilasters planned for the wings, a change that broke the rhythm of the facade and gave the building a more sober appearance. The ornamentation of the central block was ingenious, however, because it integrated the windows of the top storey into the Doric entablature.[12] This device is not unlike one used by Palladio himself (for example, in the Villa Thiene in Quinto ca. 1550).

Some buildings constructed in the Atlantic region from about 1815 to 1830 also featured a frontispiece, but by then this portion of the facade had become much more important. Province House in Halifax (1811-18) is the most sophisticated example of this (Fig. 35). It consists of a rectangular building where once again the elements of the composition are concentrated in the central block. Whereas in the earlier examples the projection from the central block was modelled on a pattern frequently used by Gibbs, here there are Ionic columns supporting the central pediment in a manner much more reminiscent of the architecture of Colen Campbell and William Kent. The dimensions of the openings (smaller on the upper storey) are another reference to Palladian precepts. The projecting lateral sections of the facade, each featuring a pediment supported by pilasters, recall a device of Gibbs that we have already encountered in the Montreal court house (Fig. 31). The use of arcades is also typical of Gibbs, although in his buildings these structures are used to frame statues. On the other hand, the interior ornamentation and certain decorative elements of the facade (blind arcades and rosettes above pilasters) suggest a knowledge of the style of the Adam brothers, and thus a more recent architecture than the Palladian.

The Arts Building (1826-27) in Fredericton, New Brunswick, also illustrates the more complicated treatment that can be given to this format (Fig. 36). Unfortunately, some of the more original but also more costly elements that the architect, John Elliott Woolford, had included in his plan were eliminated by the committee overseeing construction: the cupola

was replaced with a pediment, and the iron balustrade on the cornice was omitted.[13]

During the late 1820s and 1830s, Neoclassical elements became more common. Facades continued to be composed in the Palladian manner, but their decoration became more diverse under the Neoclassical influence. Noteworthy examples are Government House in Fredericton (1826-28) and the court house in Saint John (1826-29) (Figs 37, 38).

Collectively these buildings constructed from approximately 1815 to 1830, unlike those built from 1799 to 1815, illustrate better use of design elements characteristic of the great Palladian houses: the treatment of the facade is more sophisticated, the proportions are more balanced, and there are more decorative elements. The Neoclassical influence even begins to be evident in the ornamentation. In relation to buildings constructed at the beginning of the century, these mark a new stage in the evolution of public architecture. They show the architect's desire to build permanent structures of a certain scale while remaining, of course, within the limits imposed by the committee overseeing construction.

This type of design, with some variations, was popular throughout much of the nineteenth century. Province House in Charlottetown (1843-48), designed by Isaac Smith, is a late example (Fig. 39). A portico supported by four columns has replaced the former arrangement of a pediment applied to the facade and supported by pilasters.

A second architectural formula associated with the Palladian influence was that of the central block framed by lower side wings. This formula was much less popular than the preceding one, and the manner in which it was applied varied. It was given its most sumptuous expression in the Governor's House in Halifax (1800-1807) (Fig. 40). The Charlottetown court house (1811) was by contrast a very small building, but it featured the same arrangement (Fig. 41).

Some buildings combined lateral wings with a section projecting forward from the central block. The first Province House in Fredericton (1802) and Dalhousie College in Halifax (1820) both featured lateral wings framing a central block with a frontispiece projecting from the facade.

The use of lateral wings remained popular until the end of the 1840s (Figs 42-44). Upper

Canada College in York (1829-31), built by J.G. Chewett, is a late example (Fig. 42). The plan of this building is based on a hierarchical room arrangement: the offices, prayer rooms and classrooms are located in the central block, whereas the living quarters are situated in the wings.

A third group of buildings constructed rather late (between the 1830s and the 1850s) shows the durability of another architectural formula popularized by Palladianism. The compact and almost square design of these buildings is reminiscent of certain Palladian villas (Fig. 5). Their facade consists of a monumental portico and a raised or rusticated basement. Some examples are the Colonial Building in St. John's, Newfoundland (1847-50) (Fig. 45), the Customs Building in Montreal (1836) (Fig. 46), and numerous court houses scattered throughout Nova Scotia (Fig. 47) and especially New Brunswick.

At times, the influence of Palladian architecture on public buildings was limited to ornamentation. Thus a group of buildings constructed by the military, which varied widely in structure but were primarily utilitarian in function, featured Palladian decorative motifs. These buildings illustrate a desire to add a harmonious note to structures designed to accommodate fairly simple functions (warehouses, guard stations). They undoubtedly helped to popularize some aspects of the Palladian style. Noteworthy among them are the Prescott Gate in Quebec City (1797) the upper part of which was ornamented with a Venetian window surmounted by a pediment,[14] and the guard station of the Château Saint-Louis on Place d'Armes in Quebec City (1814), the central portion of which was surmounted by a pediment.[15] The wooden barracks in Fredericton (1815-16) featured small triangular pediments reminiscent of those on more significant buildings. Similarly, the military residences in Halifax (1826) illustrated the integration of certain Palladian elements into a primarily functional structure.

Palladianism also exerted an influence on small, commercial buildings (hotels, stores and banks) (Fig. 48). With their rectangular shape, symmetrical openings and hipped roofs, these buildings were in the great tradition of British classicism. However, their classical ornamentation, consisting of Doric pediments and Venetian windows, was Palladian inspired.

These buildings recall the small houses given wide exposure in several architectural treatises of the Palladian period, particularly those of James Gibbs and Robert Morris.

Another public building that adopted the form of British classical houses was the Governor's House in Charlottetown. Constructed in 1834 by Isaac Smith, Henry Smith and Nathan Wright, this elegant wooden building had a roof and an architectural form typical of British classicism. But its monumental portico, which stood at ground level and was surmounted by a pediment, was a mixture of Palladian and Neoclassical elements.

Finally, the Palladian style was also influential, particularly in Quebec, on various older public buildings that were to be remodelled. This influence was largely confined to the ornamentation, as noted regarding religious architecture. Thus, when the Château Saint-Louis in Quebec City was remodelled in 1808-12, it was given pediments, Venetian windows and oval windows, all typical of Palladian architecture.

As mentioned previously the circular form was greatly favoured by Palladio and subsequently by the English Palladian architects. Although the latter seldom used it, they considered it to be both the most perfect form and the form most suitable for temples. They used it occasionally for small, ornamental buildings. In addition to preparing two circular designs for St. Martin-in-the-Fields, Gibbs had the Radcliffe Library at Oxford (1739-42) built according to a circular design. He also provided plans and elevations for summerhouses in the form of circular temples (*Book of Architecture*, plate XXIX). Similarly, the Palladian architect Robert Morris in 1751 proposed a series of circular pavilions (*Architectural Remembrance*, plate XXIII).

It is therefore not surprising to find several circular buildings in Canada: the Halifax town clock (1801-1803); the Quebec City market (1806), designed by William Robe; and the Charlottetown market (1823), designed by John Plaw (Figs 49-51). The Halifax municipal clock was entirely within the Palladian tradition of small, ornamental buildings. The markets in Quebec City and Charlottetown likely were given a circular design because of their function, which required ample open space, rather than because of an aesthetic or stylistic consideration.

In summary, the form of Palladianism the colony adopted for its public buildings was a rather informal adaptation of the great domestic models proposed by the Palladians and more particularly by James Gibbs. Indeed, most of the examples noted were closer to the solutions of Gibbs than the much more elaborate solutions of the Burlington group; we also noted a wide use of the projecting frontispiece, a favourite device of Gibbs.

Public architecture during this period was much less marked by regional elements than was religious or domestic architecture. Generally, it tended to be fairly homogeneous, although certain buildings (such as the circular ones) were distinguished by the use of a particular design or model.

The use of Palladian models may be explained by the fact that public architecture was generally produced by the English government, under the direction of its representatives. Moreover, it was intended to have symbolic value and was therefore designed to signify a political, administrative, judicial or legislative presence. The builders therefore drew on models already familiar to them or those they found in the treatises. In the absence of "great" models of public architecture, they adapted the designs of English houses and villas.

DOMESTIC ARCHITECTURE

According to American author William H. Pierson, Jr., the majority of the large houses constructed in the American colonies after 1750 show the influence of James Gibbs and, to a lesser degree, Robert Morris.[1] Without being as categorical as Pierson regarding Gibbs's influence on Canadian architecture, we can state that this influence is evident in several houses constructed after 1780. It is particularly evident in buildings featuring a frontispiece, a device much used by Gibbs, or lateral wings framing a central block, or classical Palladian-inspired ornamentation.

The appearance of these houses followed a pattern nearly identical to the one noted in religious architecture. Newcomers (particularly merchants and administrators) who settled in the large centres introduced the new style when they built houses of a certain scale. They imitated their family home, or a house they had previously inhabited in England, Scotland or the United States. Although some of these houses were built toward the end of the 1780s, the majority were not constructed until the beginning of the nineteenth century.[2]

The commentaries left to us by travellers to this part of the world in the late eighteenth and early nineteenth centuries tell us a great deal about the appearance of these new Palladian houses. Visitors to Upper Canada at the end of the eighteenth century took scant notice of the first wooden houses built, although some commented that these buildings were inelegant. In 1795-97 Isaac Weld wrote that most of the houses in the town of Niagara were unadorned and made of wood. He added that the only noteworthy houses were those belonging to major government officials.[3] Visiting Kingston during the same period, the Duke de La Rochefoucauld-Liancourt wrote that none of the houses there were particularly well maintained.[4] Colonel Smith's house in Niagara (Fig. 59) was the only one to draw praise.[5] Judging from the comments of these travellers, it was not until the second decade of the nineteenth century that the first quality homes were built. In 1818-19 Edward Allen Talbot wrote that several judges and government officials residing in York had very elegant homes.[6] He mentioned John Strachan's house (Fig. 54) in particular.

The few travellers who visited the Atlantic region during the same period took little note of domestic architecture there. Their comments on it were mainly concerned with the material used — wood — and the various construction techniques employed.[7] It was during the 1820s that domestic architecture in the region began to arouse more favourable comment. John MacGregor wrote in 1828 that certain houses recently constructed in Charlottetown "are finished in a handsome style and have a lively and pleasing appearance."[8] He noted that in Halifax, brick houses were beginning to appear, and that these were "built and furnished in the same manner as in England; some of the houses built of wood are large and handsome, with the exterior painted white; and the inside lathed, plastered and papered in the same style as stone or brick houses."[9] He noted in particular the residence of the Duke of Kent and Admiralty House (Fig. 93).

In Quebec City at the end of the eighteenth century, several travellers remarked on the use of stone and commented that most of the urban homes built in the tradition of the French regime appeared monotonous and inelegant. Describing the parish of Batiscan in 1776, a German officer wrote that all the houses looked alike, only their dimensions differed.[10] Walter Johnstone in 1785[11] and Isaac Weld in 1795-97[12] found only a handful of elegant homes in Montreal. Of the houses in Quebec City's upper town, Weld noted that except for a few of the more recently built, most were "small, ugly, and inconvenient."[13] However, in 1806-1808 John Lambert noted that the new houses in the upper town were much better constructed than the older ones.[14]

Again, it was mainly the houses constructed during the second decade of the nineteenth century that elicited favourable comment. In 1818-19 Talbot wrote that the houses recently constructed on the former outskirts of Montreal showed a definite improvement in the taste of the builders.[15] He added that these few interesting houses did not enhance the appearance of the city; rather, they drew attention to the inferior appearance of the houses around them.[16]

Passing through Montreal in 1819, Benjamin Silliman noted that the city had a European appearance owing to the use of stone in construction. He praised the qualities of this material and noted disapprovingly that on the outskirts of Montreal there were several brick houses "in the anglo-american style."[17] In Quebec City, he observed that the recently constructed houses were "very handsome and in the modern style."[18]

These comments on domestic architecture of the late eighteenth and early nineteenth centuries raise several interesting points. First, apparently travellers were very attentive to the type of material used in the construction of these houses. Wood was seen as uninteresting and was often associated, particularly in the eighteenth century, with modest, inelegant buildings. Stone also aroused unfavourable comment; houses made of it were criticized as appearing somber and heavy. Only Silliman saw advantages in its use.

Generally, houses built in the eighteenth century, whether stone or wood, attracted very little attention from travellers. The appearance of the first buildings showing "English" or "Anglo-American" influence, on the other hand, elicited much more favourable, sometimes laudatory comments, probably because this type of architecture was more familiar to these travellers, most of whom were of English origin. These buildings were described as in the "modern" style, or built in a manner similar to that in England. These new structures were also seen as marking a definite improvement in building quality.

Finally, the travellers' accounts confirm several of the conclusions suggested by our survey, which revealed very few Palladian-inspired houses built before the beginning of the nineteenth century. It was during the second decade of the new century in York, at the end of that decade in Quebec City and Montreal, and throughout the same decade in the Atlantic provinces that many such houses began to be built. Travellers' accounts attest to this chronology and this geographical distribution and confirm that English-style houses began to appear during this period. The survey also revealed that the majority of these houses were located in the large centres or their immediate environs; they were built by wealthy people, generally of English origin, who occupied positions in administration, government, commerce or the judiciary. The travellers' comments confirm these findings.

The Palladian influence on domestic architecture was reflected in two types of structures characteristic of the great English houses: one featured a central frontispiece surmounted by a pediment (for example, Figs 52, 69, 86), and the other had lateral wings framing the main body of the building (for example, Figs 61, 72, 90). On smaller buildings, the Palladian influence was reflected in the ornamentation (Venetian window, door framed by pilasters or by an architrave surmounted by a small pediment), which was applied to a structure whose form was derived from the British classical tradition (for example, Figs 65, 78, 99). This classical ornamentation inspired by Palladianism was to be gradually adopted and assimilated into various regional traditions (Figs 68, 85, 98).

Ontario

Curiously, it is in Ontario that the greatest number of Palladian houses are found, whereas there appear to have been very few Palladian churches and public buildings there. One of the most interesting as well as the earliest manifestations of the Palladian influence on domestic architecture appeared at the end of the eighteenth century, when houses began to feature a frontispiece projecting from their facade (Figs 52, 53). This projecting frontispiece surmounted by a pediment accentuated the building's central vertical axis and emphasized the entrance, according to the rule established by Palladio and popularized by Gibbs. William Dickson's house in Niagara (1787) and Maryville Lodge in York (1794) are the earliest examples of this device in Ontario.

Although it appeared fairly early, this design nevertheless was used for much of the first half of the nineteenth century. Originally it was associated with large dwellings. In York, in particular, it was found on brick houses constructed for prominent people (Figs 54, 55). As early as the beginning of the nineteenth century, it was used as well for buildings of more modest proportions. It was also during this period that some such houses began to feature Neoclassical motifs as well as modifications in the treatment of the frontispiece (Figs 56-58).

The addition of lateral wings to the central block of the house represented a second Palladian compositional feature. It was associated with houses of a certain scale constructed for wealthy people (Figs 59-61). The residence of Robert Reynolds (1816-19) in Amherstburg was unique in the colony (Fig. 61). Much more than other houses, this one recalled the large country houses found in England or in the American south, probably because its side wings were sizable and were linked by a long corridor to the building's central block.

The device of a main block balanced by two wings was to remain popular throughout much of the nineteenth century. It was even incorporated in Greek Revival architecture, as in the case of Eliakim Barnum's house in Grafton (1817). The latter consisted of a central block flanked by two lower side wings, but here the central block had a basically vertical rather than horizontal thrust, as well as new ornamentation (an arcade), which gave the building an entirely different appearance. The central portion of the building assumed considerable importance, unlike in the first Palladian compositions.

Various architectural treatises of the Palladian period popularized another type of house whose form was derived from the great British classical tradition inherited from the seventeenth century, but whose ornamentation was borrowed from Palladian architecture. Such houses were much more modest both in size and appearance than those mentioned previously, and this accounts for their immense popularity in the colonies. Robert Morris[19] and James Gibbs[20] included models of such houses in their treatises. In addition, some highly interesting models were proposed by Asher Benjamin, the American author who at the beginning of his career helped to disseminate certain elements of Palladian architecture.[21]

It was in Ontario that the greatest number of such houses were constructed throughout the entire first half of the nineteenth century (Fig. 62). They tended to have the following characteristics: a rectangular form; two storeys with a slightly raised basement; five openings on the front, including a Venetian window above the central door; a front door framed by side lights or small windows; and finally, on occasion, a small portico. The Venetian window was sometimes omitted or replaced with a flat-topped window larger than the others. The front door was usually the most ornamented part of the facade.

The Palladians attributed great importance to their front doors. Robert Morris considered that porticos and porches lent grace and nobility to a building and that the pediment was the best means of covering a portico.[22] On most of his buildings the tops of the doors were flat, with entablatures or pediments for ornamentation. By contrast, Batty Langley offered examples of round-arched doors.[23] Asher Benjamin also proposed doors with semicircular tops framed by pediments and pilasters, as well as doors with side lights and semicircular transoms.[24] Finally, certain treatises on Palladian architecture suggested another device occasionally used by Palladio, namely a main door with small, separate windows on either side.

Reflecting this diversity, several types of doors are found in Ontario that illustrate — often in a very informal manner — the influence of these models: doors ornamented with a semicircular transom, others framed by small side windows, and still others surmounted by a small Doric or Ionic pediment (Figs 62-67). Particularly noteworthy are certain one-storey houses, generally built of stone or more rarely of wood, that constitute a category of houses typical of Ontario and feature classical ornamentation around the front door (Fig. 68). Despite their small size, several of these houses show evidence of a concern for harmonious proportions and refined ornamentation. One can only be charmed by the beauty of some of these buildings.

Thus Ontario offers a considerable variety of houses that directly or indirectly relate to the Palladian tradition. The monumental houses constructed between 1780 and 1820, generally by the influential and wealthy, are authentically Palladian in their elevations and ornamentation, and they reflect — often faithfully — the great models of this style. There are also several small houses that feature some of the more striking Palladian motifs, including the classical ornamentation of the door. Whereas the monumental houses were generally made of brick or stone, these smaller ones were usually either stone or wood.

Quebec

It was in Quebec City, at the end of the eighteenth century, that the first Palladian-inspired houses appeared. Although these were only isolated examples of the new style, they were sufficiently representative that their role in its dissemination in Quebec cannot be neglected. Most of the great Palladian houses, however, were built at the beginning of the nineteenth century in Montreal and Quebec City. As in Ontario, the Palladian influence was expressed by a frontispiece projecting from the facade, lateral wings, and ornamentation. In addition to these few, more elegant buildings, there were also houses whose form was derived from the British classical tradition but whose ornamentation was Palladian.

The manner in which these new architectural models were introduced was here again closely tied to the arrival of the new society of English and American origin, and its gradual establishment. Nonetheless, the existence of deeply rooted architectural traditions added another dimension to the introduction of this style into Quebec's domestic architecture, because it entailed more modifications and adaptations than in the other regions.

The formula of the central frontispiece projecting from the facade does not seem to have been as popular as in Ontario, for we found few houses with this feature. Apparently they were introduced in Quebec City at the end of the eighteenth century (Fig. 69). Subsequently they began to appear in the Montreal area during the second decade of the nineteenth century, as seen in the house of Judge Louis-Charles Foucher (constructed ca. 1820, demolished in 1939).

The Palladian influence was also evident in a type of house consisting of a central block flanked by either lateral wings or pavilions linked by long corridors (Figs 70-74). The facade of the central block of some of these houses sometimes featured a central frontispiece (Figs 70, 71). In some cases, the lateral wings were added to the buildings some time after the construction of the central block (Fig. 73). Because of their layout, these houses required considerable space and therefore were built on large properties. In terms of their site, proportions, layout and ornamentation, they were the direct descendents of the great English country houses. It was in Quebec that we found the greatest number of these houses.

In Quebec the Palladian influence was also evident in classical ornamentation that drew on the Palladian vocabulary, but that was applied to houses whose form was derived from the great British classical tradition. Numerous houses constructed throughout much of the first half of the nineteenth century illustrate this phenomenon (Figs 75-82).

As in the other regions settled by Loyalist immigrants, this type of building may have been introduced into Quebec via the United States, for example, the two country houses built by Sir John Johnson at Argenteuil and St-Mathias were imitations of his family home, Mount Johnson, in New York State (Figs 77-79). It is not surprising, then, to discover similarities between various Palladian-inspired houses in Quebec and houses in the United States. In many cases, the former were constructed by persons who had settled in Quebec after a stay in the United States, where they were exposed to this type of architecture.

Several authors have noted that the basic lines of traditional houses were altered following the introduction of the new models.[25] Even though it is difficult to establish a definite link between these changes and the arrival of the Palladian style, the angle of the roofs gradually became less steep, the type of roof changed (hipped roofs became more common), the very structure of houses became higher and also more harmonious, and the spatial arrangement of openings became more symmetrical.

Similarly, the new buildings undoubtedly served to create a taste for more heavily ornamented facades and a more harmonious ordering of architectural elements. Thus during this period several urban houses began to feature a new type of ornamentation concentrated around the front door: generally, this took the form of semicircular transoms, entablatures and Doric and Ionic mouldings. In addition, the openings were sometimes arranged according to the Palladian rule that windows on the top storey had to be small and square (Figs 83-85). Some urban houses, especially in Quebec City, even adopted the squat, compact form characteristic of British classical buildings.

Thus the Palladian influence on domestic architecture in Quebec found expression in three basic forms. First, there were the rather elegant and monumental houses imitating the great Palladian models. This was a fairly small group of buildings, but their impact should not be underestimated. Second, there were more numerous smaller houses, which combined a structure derived from British classicism with Palladian-inspired classical ornamentation. This combination likely came from the United States. Finally, there were traditional houses which were embellished with the more striking decorative motifs of the new style, or which underwent more significant changes, affecting their fenestration or roofing or even their proportions or form.

Atlantic Provinces

Compared with Ontario or even Quebec, the Atlantic region offers very few great Palladian-inspired houses. However, it contains several houses combining the British classical format with Palladian-inspired classical ornamentation. Such buildings are found mainly in Nova Scotia and New Brunswick.

The building type featuring a central frontispiece appeared earliest, as in Quebec and Ontario. Here again it was used for homes belonging to wealthy people of English origin, often involved in the political, administrative or social life of the colony. The Naval Commissioner's House in Halifax (ca. 1785) is probably the earliest example of this type of building (Fig. 86). Its front and rear feature a frontispiece surmounted by a pediment and adorned with a Venetian window. Unlike most of the buildings in the other regions, this one is made of wood, a typical building material in this part of the country.

Several houses situated in the vicinity of Pictou and Halifax also employ this formula, albeit much more conventionally, because only the front of the building features a frontispiece. In some cases, pilasters are used to frame it and support the central pediment, emphasizing the central part of the building.

Mount Uniacke (1813-15), the house of John Uniacke situated near Halifax, is especially interesting (Fig. 87). This house does not feature the projecting frontispiece popularized by Gibbs, but rather employs a device favoured by Palladio, namely the monumental portico supported by columns. Thus the facade of this house features a large, projecting pediment supported by four columns. The basement is raised, as proposed by Palladio, and access to the main entrance is via lateral stairways. Also according to Palladianism, all the elements of the composition converge on the central portion of the building. Mount Uniacke is one of the rare buildings in the colony to use a monumental portico, as in certain mansions in the American South.

The Atlantic region features several houses that illustrate the formula of lateral wings flanking a central block (Figs 88-91). Generally these houses are a very simple, austere design compared with those in other regions.

There is also a fairly large group of houses combining the compact form derived from the British classical tradition with Palladian ornamentation. Most are located in New Brunswick, although several are found in Nova Scotia.

Acacia Grove at Starr's Point is a fine example of such architecture (Fig. 92). It is a rectangular building with five openings on its facade, and a hipped roof flanked by two chimneys, a raised basement and a small pediment over the front door. Its forms are balanced and harmonious, and its overall effect is one of monumentality, which is lacking in the vernacular adaptations that are examined later. Acacia Grove, like several other houses of the same type, draws on models presented in the treatises of Morris, Gibbs and Benjamin (Figs 7, 8).

The houses in this category were constructed between 1810 and 1830 (Figs 93, 95, 96). Whether stone or wood, they were rectangular and generally had a hipped roof and five openings on the front (although there were several with three openings). The end of the second decade of the century saw a tendency toward greater monumentality, (three storeys, larger openings). It was during these years that the semicircular transom gradually gave way to the semielliptical one, marking the arrival of Neoclassical ornamentation.

Parallel to this relatively refined and elaborate architecture, many vernacular dwellings were constructed, generally wood. Although most of them were not characterized by any specific stylistic influence, several were adorned with decorative motifs borrowed from the more monumental houses (Figs 97-101). These houses date from throughout the first half of the nineteenth century and in many cases represent a combination of the influence of vernacular architecture, the British classical tradition and Palladianism.

Although there were fewer Palladian-inspired mansions in this region than in Ontario or Quebec, many smaller houses showed the influence of this style. Several featured highly original adaptations of some of its motifs. In some cases stylistic details were rendered in a highly delicate and refined manner, probably owing to the use of wood as a construction material.

What conclusions may be drawn from this overview of the influence of Palladianism on domestic architecture in the colony? First, this influence was manifested in the design of several mansions, generally constructed by people from England, Scotland or the United States who wished to imitate familiar architectural models. Some of these mansions featured the central frontispiece popularized by Gibbs, or the use of lateral wings. Others combined a form derived from the great British classical tradition with Palladian-inspired classical ornamentation. These houses were generally situated in the major cities or their immediate environs and were primarily notable for their monumentality, their use of harmonious forms and spatial relationships and their highly methodical use of the classical vocabulary.

The presence of this domestic architecture, innovative in its form, elevations and ornamentation, was to influence the architecture of smaller, more modest houses. It was also to affect traditional domestic architecture — both the well-established architecture of Quebec and the architecture introduced by American or British immigrants, as in Ontario and the Atlantic region. Here the Palladian influence was expressed in the decorative treatment of doors, particularly in the use of small pediments, pilasters, orders and semicircular transoms.

The introduction of this architectural style was closely linked with the arrival and establishment of a new society of British origin. Indeed, several of the Palladian-inspired mansions belonged to merchants, administrators or political figures newly arrived in the colony.

Compared with public and religious architecture, domestic architecture was characterized by a greater freedom and more modifications of the Palladian vocabulary. Various factors may explain this situation: the modes of dissemination of the style, the time lag between developments in England and in the colony and various constraints specific to the colony. Furthermore, whereas political motives or considerations of prestige often dictated the use of Palladian models in religious and public architecture, these factors did not affect domestic architecture, or were at least much less influential and did not prevent a somewhat more imaginative treatment. The administrative controls exerted over religious and public architecture were almost entirely absent, and this made it possible for each builder to modify and interpret the style more freely. Finally, in many cases regional traditions either already well-established or brought in by various groups of immigrants slowed the dissemination of the style. Generally, regarding large houses as well as smaller ones, Palladianism conveyed a more "classical" appearance, primarily through the introduction of a new decorative vocabulary and through the application of the principles of harmony, symmetry and balance.

CONCLUSION

The introduction of Palladian-inspired architectural models is closely linked with a period in our history characterized by the arrival and establishment of a new society of British origin and the creation of new institutions (political, judicial, religious and administrative). During this period, the newcomers immigrating here from England, Scotland and the United States brought with them a concept of architecture that had become firmly established in England during the first half of the eighteenth century, when Palladianism was the official style associated with the aristocracy and the social elite. Rapidly popularized through the architectural treatises, this style had been applied in modified form to various types of buildings. Naturally, the immigrants brought some of these architectural models, which were already familiar to them, when they came to the new land.

This study on the influence exerted by Palladian architecture in Canada shows that it was the religious buildings and public structures that most faithfully incorporated certain aspects of this style. The introduction of Palladian models in the colony was initially linked with the establishment of the Anglican Church, as shown by the construction of St. Paul's Church in Halifax and Holy Trinity Cathedral in Quebec City. Subsequently, this new architectural style, which was not without its charms, influenced the small churches of various denominations, primarily in the decorative elements of the style they adopted.

The architecture of Palladian-inspired public buildings tended to be uniform and homogeneous. The control exerted by government authorities was relatively constant and resulted in the establishment of a fairly standardized building type. Therefore, it was often the public buildings that were the most faithful to the great domestic models of Palladian architecture, as seen in Province House in Halifax and the court house in Saint John.

Whereas in England Palladianism was a domestic style, in the colonies it was precisely in the area of domestic architecture that it was least influential, because conditions were not propitious to the construction of very large homes. The Palladian influence often had to be grafted onto existing traditions or adapted to the constraints of the colonial setting (climate, budgets, materials available, manpower). It therefore took various forms in the different regions. The most popular stylistic elements and the most widely copied were the Venetian window, the pediment, the architrave and the transom over the door.

As in England, the Palladian style established in Canada certain standards of taste that remained in effect for many years. Its influence was primarily manifested in a greater use of the classical vocabulary and a taste for more harmonious proportions. This Palladian heritage remained strong throughout much of the nineteenth century, particularly in the manner in which facades were organized and ornamented. Moreover, the Palladian layouts, compositions and classical ornamentation paved the way for the Neoclassical models, which in many cases were much more elaborate and varied.

ENDNOTES

Introduction

1 For example, in 1819 Silliman described the court house in Quebec City as "a modern stone building." Dr. Benjamin Silliman, A Tour to Quebec in the Autumn of 1819 (London: Richard Phillips, 1822), p. 111.

2 For example, in 1821 Howison said of Montreal, "...Its Suburbs and Outskirts are embellished by numerous villas built in the English style...." John Howison, Sketches of Upper Canada, Domestic, Local, and Characteristic... (Edinburgh: Olive and Boyd, 1821), p. 6.

3 Silliman wrote of the outskirts of Montreal, "...and we were sorry to see even a few private houses in the suburbs of Montreal built of brick in the anglo-american style." Dr. Benjamin Silliman, op. cit., p. 117.

4 The Oxford English Dictionary (Oxford: Clarendon Press, 1961), s.v. "Palladian."

5 J. George Hodgins, The School House; its Architecture, External and Internal Arrangements (Toronto: Lovell and Gibson, 1857), p. 5.

6 John Summerson, Architecture in Britain 1530 to 1830, 5th ed. (Harmondsworth: Penguin, 1969) (hereafter cited as Architecture in Britain 1530-1830), p. 211.

7 Rudolf Wittkower, Palladio and English Palladianism (London: Thames and Hudson, ca. 1974) (hereafter cited as Palladio and English Palladianism), pp. 155-76.

8 R.S. Peabody, "Georgian Houses of New England," American Architect and Building News, Vol. 2 (Oct. 1877), pp. 338-39; Vol. 3 (Feb. 1878), pp. 54-55. See also Frank J. Roos, Writings on Early American Architecture. An Annotated List of Books and Articles on Architecture Constructed Before 1860 in the Eastern Half of the United States (Columbus: Ohio State University Press, 1943).

9 Marcus Whiffen, American Architecture Since 1780. A Guide to the Styles (Cambridge: MIT Press, 1969), pp. 160-61.

10 R.S. Peabody, op. cit., p. 338.

11 Ibid.

12 Harold Donaldson Eberlein, The Architecture of Colonial America (New York: Johnson Reprint, 1968), reprint 1915 ed., p. 10.

13 Marcus Whiffen, op. cit., pp. 8-13.

14 William H. Pierson, Jr., American Buildings and Their Architects. The Colonial and Neoclassical Styles (New York: Doubleday, 1970), pp. 111-56.

15 Eric R. Arthur, Toronto. No Mean City (Toronto: University of Toronto Press, 1964), pp. 24-25.

16 Ramsay Traquair, The Old Architecture of Quebec (Toronto: MacMillan, 1947), pp. 68, 73-74.

17 Marion MacRae, The Ancestral Roof. Domestic Architecture of Upper Canada (Toronto: Clarke, Irwin, 1963), p. 36.

18 Author Alan Gowans also uses this term, but in a wider context. Alan Gowans, Looking at Architecture in Canada (Toronto: Oxford University Press, 1958), pp. 63-69.

The Palladian Movement in England

1 John Summerson, Architecture in Britain 1530-1830, pp. 181-245.

2 Rudolf Wittkower, Palladio and English Palladianism; idem, Architectural Principles in the Age of Humanism (London: Academy Editions, 1974), (hereafter cited as Architectural Principles), reprint 4th ed.

3 James S. Ackerman, Palladio (Harmondsworth: Penguin, 1966).

4 Palladio's treatise also appeared in later editions, including one in 1581 and another in 1601. During the seventeenth century various attempts were made to translate parts of it. However, these translations were always incomplete, and indeed they were sometimes translations of Dutch or Flemish translations of the original. Rudolf Wittkower, Palladio and English Palladianism, pp. 76-77.

5 The architectural treatise of Vitruvius, dating from the reign of Caesar Augustus, is considered to be the only one to have been passed down from anti-

quity. It deals with the principles of symmetry, harmony and proportion, as well as the style and proportions appropriate for private buildings. It describes the Ionic, Doric and Corinthian orders, and it mentions the Tuscan order. It was Vitruvius who initiated the practice of personalizing the orders; this practice was taken up by the architects of the Renaissance. Vitruvius's treatise was first published in 1486.

6   De Re Aedificatoria was the first great treatise of the Renaissance. It was published in 1485. It was Alberti who added the Composite order to the four orders previously described by Vitruvius.

7   Rudolf Wittkower, Palladio and English Palladianism, p. 111.

8   A. Lytton Sells, The Paradise of Travellers. The Italian Influence on Englishmen in the Seventeenth Century (Bloomington: Indiana University, 1964), p. 75.

9   Only Sir Roger Pratt and John Webb attempted to explore some of the ideas advanced by Inigo Jones.

10 John Summerson, Georgian London (London: Pleiades, 1945) (hereafter cited as Georgian London), pp. 20-21.

11 A second volume appeared in 1717 and an additional volume in 1725.

12 We know, for example, that in 1715, Richard Boyle, third Earl of Burlington, remodelled Burlington House in the Palladian spirit.

13 Contrary to what is generally written, the first volume of Leoni's translation of Palladio appeared in 1716, even though it bears the date 1715. The second, third and fourth volumes appeared successively in 1717, 1718 and 1719-20. Rudolf Wittkower, Palladio and English Palladianism, pp. 80-84.

14 For a translation faithful to the Italian original, it was necessary to wait until 1738 for Isaac Ware's Four Books of Architecture, published at Burlington's instigation. Indeed, Ware's purpose as stated in his preface was to do justice to Palladio, contrary to what had been done in the two previous translations. Ware was referring to that of Leoni, which had appeared in 1716, and that of Edward Hoppus and Benjamin Cole, which had appeared in 1733-35. The latter work

was inspired by Leoni's volumes 2, 3 and 4 and by volume 1 which Colen had published in 1728. Rudolf Wittkower, Palladio and English Palladianism, pp. 86-88.

15 In a chapter entitled "English literature on architecture," Rudolf Wittkower provides an excellent overview of sixteenth and seventeenth century English publications. Rudolph Wittkower, Palladio and English Palladianism, pp. 95-112.

16 John Harris, Georgian Country Houses (Feltham: Country Life, 1968), p. 15.

17 The Isaac Ware translation was the first to conform to the Italian original. Rudolf Wittkower, Palladio and English Palladianism, p. 88.

18 Robert Morris, in Lectures on Architecture Consisting of Rules Founded on Harmonick and Arithmetical Proportions in Buildings (London: J. Brindley, 1734) (hereafter cited as Lectures on Architecture), took up some of the criticisms made by Ralph. But elsewhere he denounced others, such as Ralph's criticism of Grosvenor Square.

19 Robert Morris, The Architectural Remembrancer Being a Collection of New and Useful Designs of Ornamental Buildings and Decorations for Parks, Gardens, Woods, & C. (Farnborough: Green International, 1971), p. iv.

20 See John Summerson, Architecture in Britain 1530-1830, pp. 205-10; Rudolf Wittkower, Palladio and English Palladianism, pp. 104-5; John Harris, op. cit., p. 31.

21 John Summerson, Architecture in Britain 1530-1830, pp. 192-204, 222-26.

22 Rudolf Wittkower, Architectural Principles, p. 77.

23 Ibid., in designing his palazzos and public buildings (for example, the Palazzo Porto-Colleoni), Palladio adapted a formula used by Bramante and Raphael in the sixteenth century in a group of buildings constructed in Rome.

24 John Summerson, Architecture in Britain 1530-1830, p. 222.

25 From religious architecture, Palladio borrowed the portico surmounted by a central pediment and adapted it to domestic architecture. R. Wittkower, Architecture Principles, p. 74.

26 John Summerson, Georgian London, p. 95.

Introduction of the Palladian Style into the Colony

1   R.V. Harris, The Church of St. Paul in Halifax, N.S. (Toronto: Ryerson, 1949), p. 15.
2   F.C. Würtele, "The English Cathedral of Quebec," Transactions of the Literary and Historical Society of Quebec (1889-91), No. 20, 1891, pp. 76-84.
3   Quebec. Ministère des Affaires culturelles, Gérard Morisset collection; folio "Ancien palais de justice, Québec," Jonathan Sewell to William Hall, Sept. 2, 1799.
4   Catalogue of English and French Books in the Quebec Library (n.p.: n.p., 1785).
5   It is most probably Isaac Ware's 1738 edition because this is the one mentioned in the 1792 and 1796 catalogues.
6   "Catalogue de livres à vendre à l'imprimerie à Québec," La Gazette de Québec, 6 Sept. 1787, p. 4.
7   Indeed, some of these books were probably available under the French regime. Quebec City, Bibliothèque du séminaire de Québec, Sem 4, No. 128, report on books left by Abbé Mathurin Jacrau Aug. 30, 1764, given Nov. 15, 1770; ibid., inventory made by Dudevant, 1782.
8   Quebec, Archives nationales du Québec à Québec, records of notary R. Lelièvre, inventory, May 30, 1808.
9   Quebec City, Archives du séminaire de Québec, polygraphie 19, No. 59, will of Thomas Baillairgé, 5 April 1848.
10 Although there are excellent studies on the history and development of England's Royal Military Academy, none examines in detail the training received by the cadets, or more particularly their architectural training. Among these studies are the following: F.G. Guggisberg, "The shop." The Story of the Royal Military Academy (London: Cassell, 1902); Whithworth Porter, History of the Corps of Royal Engineers (London: Longman, Green, 1889), 2 vols.; Oliver Frederick Gillilan Hogg, The Royal Arsenal: its Background, Origin and Subsequent History (London: Oxford University Press, 1963), 2 vols. Records of the Royal Military Academy 1741-1892 (Woolwich: F.J. Cattermole, 1892) were most informative on this subject.
11 F.G. Guggisberg, op. cit., p. 25.
12 Records of the Royal Military Academy 1741-1892, p. 12.
13 Ibid., p. 45.
14 Ibid., p. 58.
15 Msgr Olivier Maurault, "Un professeur d'architecture en 1828," L'art au Canada, (Montreal), 1929, pp. 93-113.
16 Gérard Morisset, "Une figure inconnue Jérôme Demers," La Patrie (Montreal), 22 March 1953, pp. 36-37.
17 Luc Noppen, "Le rôle de l'abbé Jérôme Demers dans l'élaboration d'une architecture néo-classique au Québec," Annales d'histoire de l'art canadien (Montreal), Vol. 2, No. 1 (summer 1975), pp. 19-33. Idem, "Le renouveau architectural proposé par Thomas Baillairgé au Québec de 1820 à 1850," Ph.D. dissertation, Toulouse-Le Mirail University, France, 1976. We are especially indebted to Mr. Noppen for his study on the sources of Demers's Précis d'architecture and François Baillairgé's influence on it.
18 Premier tome de l'architecture (Frédéric Morel, Paris, 1567). This book is in the Bibliothèque du séminaire de Québec in Quebec City.
19 Quebec City, Archives du séminaire de Québec, M-131, tablette 4, Précis d'architecture de Jérôme Demers, 1828, article 413.
20 Ibid., article 246.

Religious Architecture

1   William H. Pierson, Jr., op. cit., pp. 111-56.
2   Harold Donaldson Eberlein, op. cit., pp. 99-165, 205-35.
3   John Lambert, Travels Through Lower Canada and the United States of North America in the Years 1806, 1807 and 1808 (London: Richard Phillips, 1810), Vol. 1, p. 53.
4   George Heriot, Travels Through the Can-

adas, Containing a Description of the Picturesque Scenery on Some of the Rivers and Lakes (London: Richard Phillips, 1807), p. 69.

5   Edward Allen Talbot, Five Year's Residence in the Canadas: Including a Tour Through Part of the United States of America in the Year 1823 (London: Longman, Hurst, Rees, Orme, Brown and Green, 1824) (hereafter cited as Five Year's Residence in the Canadas), Vol. 1, p. 54.

6   Ibid., p. 69.

7   Dr. Benjamin Silliman, op. cit., p. 118.

8   Patrick Campbell, Travels in the Interior Inhabited Parts of North America. In the Years 1791 and 1792 (Edinburgh: J. Guthrie, 1793), p. 21.

9   J. MacGregor, Historical and Descriptive Sketches of the Maritime Colonies of British America (Wakefield: S.R. Publishers, 1968), reprint 1828 ed., p. 138.

10 E.T. Coke, A Subaltern's Furlough: Descriptive of Scenes in Various Parts of the United States, Upper and Lower Canada, New-Brunswick, and Nova Scotia, During the Summer and Autumn of 1832 (London: Saunders and Otley, 1833), p. 410.

11 R.V. Harris, op. cit., p. 15.

12 In the churches designed by English architect Christopher Wren, the steeple is located in a projection in front of the facade. James Gibbs was the first to put the steeple on the roof.

13 Andrea Palladio, The Four Books of Architecture (New York: Dover, 1965), Vol. 4, Chap. 2, pp. 81-82.

14 Heritage Trust of Nova Scotia, Founded Upon a Rock; Historic Buildings of Halifax and Vicinity Standing in 1967, (Halifax: Heritage Trust of Nova Scotia, 1967) (hereafter cited as Founded Upon a Rock), p. 14. Arthur W. Wallace, An Album of Drawings of Early Buildings in Nova Scotia (Halifax: Heritage Trust of Nova Scotia, 1976), pp. 18-20.

15 Luc Noppen, Les églises du Québec (1600-1850) (Quebec City: Fides, 1977) (hereafter cited as Les églises du Québec (1600-1850)), p. 24.

16 Ibid., pp. 27-28.

17 The census of Quebec City carried out in 1818 by Curé Joseph Signay enumerated 3503 Protestants within a total population of 16,008 (not including the garrison or the Château St-Louis). "Recensement de la ville de Québec en 1818 par le curé Joseph Signay," comp. Abbé H. Provost (Quebec City: Société historique de Québec, 1976), Cahiers d'histoire, No. 29, p. 278.

18 A.J.H. Richardson, "Guide to the Architecturally and Historically most Significant Buildings of the Old City of Québec with a Biographical Dictionary of Architects and Builders and Illustrations," Bulletin of the Association for Preservation Technology, Ottawa, Vol. 2, Nos. 3-4 (1970), p. 69.

19 Arthur G. Doughty, Report of the Work of the Public Archives for the Years 1914 and 1915 (Ottawa: J. de L. Taché, 1916), pp. 253-54.

20 Most of the works mentioned by Major Robe were available in Quebec City at the time. See "Introduction of the Palladian Style into the Colony."

21 F.C. Würtele, op. cit., pp. 77-84.

22 Jean Trudel, William Berczy. La Famille Woolsey (Ottawa: National Gallery of Canada, 1976), p. 22.

23 Luc Noppen, Les églises du Québec, (1600-1850), pp. 39-44.

24 Ibid., p. 39; the Connefroy plan is an adaptation of the Jesuit plan.

25 John R. Porter and Léopold Désy, "L'ancienne chapelle des récollets de Trois-Rivières," Bulletin No. 18 (Ottawa: National Gallery of Canada, 1971).

26 Luc Noppen, Les églises du Québec (1600-1850), pp. 39-44.

Public Architecture

1   John Summerson, Georgian London, p. 95.

2   George Heriot, op. cit., p. 66.

3   John Palmer, Journal of Travels in the United States of North America and in Lower Canada Performed in the Year 1817 (London: Sherwood, Neely, and Jones, 1818), p. 214.

4   Edward Allen Talbot, Five Years' Residence in the Canadas, Vol. 1, pp. 46, 66.

5   Two travellers mentioning the court

house were George Heriot, op. cit., p. 69, and John Lambert, op. cit., Vol. 1, p. 50. Lambert (op. cit., p. 51) was also among those mentioning the Château St-Louis.

6 Francis Hall, Travels in Canada and the United States in 1816 and 1817 (London: Longman, Hurst, Rees, Orme and Brown, 1818), p. 75.

7 Dr. Benjamin Silliman, op. cit., p. 111.

8 John MacGregor, op. cit., p. 132. See also E.T. Coke, op. cit., p. 410.

9 Thomas Chandler Haliburton, A General Description of Nova Scotia (Halifax: Clement H. Belcher, 1825), p. 67.

10 E.T. Coke, op. cit., p. 376.

11 D. Karel, L. Noppen and C. Thibault, François Baillairgé et son oeuvre (1759-1830) (Quebec City: Musée du Québec, 1975), pp. 72-73.

12 Ibid.

13 University of New Brunswick, Fredericton, Harriet Irving Library Archives, documents pertaining to the Arts Building, Nos. 382-85.

14 Christina Cameron and Jean Trudel, Québec au temps de James Patterson Cockburn (Quebec City: Garneau, 1976), p. 110.

15 Ibid., p. 95.

Domestic Architecture

1 William H. Pierson, Jr., op. cit., pp. 115-30.

2 In London by this time, the great Palladian buildings had long since been superseded by Neoclassical structures. John Summerson, Architecture in Britain, 1530-1830, pp. 245-321.

3 Isaac Weld, Travels Through the States of North America and the Provinces of Upper and Lower Canada During the Years 1795, 1796 and 1797 (London: John Stockdale, 1807), Vol. 2, p. 89.

4 Duke François Alexandre Frédéric de La Rochefoucauld-Liancourt, Voyage dans les Etats-Unis d'Amérique, fait en 1795, 1796 et 1797 (Paris: DuPont 1799), Vol. 2, p. 122.

5 Ibid., p. 85.

6 Edward Allen Talbot, Five Years' Residence in the Canadas, Vol. 1, p. 101.

7 Daniel Cobb Harvey, ed., Journeys to the Islands of St. John or Prince Edward Island 1775-1832 (Toronto: MacMillan, 1955), p. 97.

8 John MacGregor, op. cit., p. 4.

9 Ibid., pp. 138-39.

10 William L. Stone, Letters of Brunswick and Hessian Officers During the American Revolution (Albany: Joel Munsell's Sons, 1891), p. 16.

11 Douglas S. Robertson, ed., An Englishman in America, 1795. Being the Diary of Joseph Hadfield (Toronto: Hunter-Rose, 1933), p. 46.

12 Isaac Weld, op. cit., Vol. 1, p. 310.

13 Ibid., p. 350.

14 John Lambert, op. cit., Vol. 1, p. 68.

15 Edward Allen Talbot, Five Years' Residence in the Canadas, p. 66.

16 Ibid., p. 75.

17 Dr. Benjamin Silliman, op. cit., p. 117.

18 Ibid.

19 Robert Morris, Rural Architecture Consisting of Regular Designs of Plans and Elevations for Buildings in the Country..., (Farnborough: Gregg International, 1971).

20 James Gibbs, A Book of Architecture Containing Designs of Buildings and Ornaments (New York: Benjamin Blom, 1968), reprint of 1st ed., 1728.

21 Asher Benjamin, The Country Builder's Assistant: Containing a Collection of New Designs of Carpentry and Architecture (Greenfield: Thomas Dickman, 1797) (hereafter cited as The Country Builder's Assistant).

22 Robert Morris, Lectures on Architecture, Lecture 7.

23 Batty Langley and Thomas Langley, The Builder's Jewel or, the Youth's Instructor and Workman's Remembrancer (London: R. Ware, 1757), Chap. 6, pp. 24-25.

24 Asher Benjamin, The Country Builder's Assistant, plate 11.

25 For example, Hélène Bédard, Maisons et églises du Québec (Quebec City: ministère des Affaires culturelles, 1972), pp. 18-28; Michel Lessard and Huguette Marquis, Encyclopédie de la maison québécoise (Montreal: Editions de l'Homme, 1971), pp. 312-54.

ILLUSTRATIONS

List of Illustrations

57   264 King Street East, Kingston, Ontario
58   320 Dibble Street, Prescott, Ontario
59   William Smith House, Niagara-on-the-Lake, Ontario
60   Alexander Fraser House, Fraserfield, Ontario
61   Belle Vue, 525 Dalhousie Street, Amherstburg, Ontario
62   Laurent Quetton de St. George House, 204 King Street East, Toronto
63   Homewood, Maitland, Ontario
64   Gladys Dudley, Maitland, Ontario
65   113 Johnson Street, Kingston, Ontario
66   126 Johnson Street, Niagara-on-the-Lake, Ontario
67   Maplelawn, 529 Richmond Road, Ottawa
68   Robert Millen House, Bay Street, Toronto
69   T.A. Coffin House, St. Louis Street, Quebec City
70   Spencer Wood, St. Louis Road, Quebec City
71   Caldwell Manor, Etchemin River, Quebec
72   Rolland Manor, 625 des Hurons Road West, St-Mathias, Quebec
73   St. Antoine Hall, 1322-1338 Torrance Street, Montreal
74   Jonathan Sewell House, 87 St. Louis Street, Quebec City
75   Monklands, 4245 Décarie Boulevard, Montreal
76   540 Salaberry Street East, Mercier, Quebec
77   Johnson Manor, St-André d'Argenteuil, Quebec
78   Johnson Manor, St-Mathias, Quebec
79   Mount Johnson, Johnstown, New York
80   William Lunn House, 4 du Parc Avenue, Montreal
81   Couillard de L'Espinay Manor, Montmagny, Quebec
82   Charles-Michel de Salaberry House, 18 Richelieu Street, Chambly, Quebec
83   51 St. Louis Street, Quebec City
84   40 Ste-Angèle Street, Quebec City
85   37 Ste-Ursule Street, Quebec City
86   Naval Commissioner's House, Halifax
87   Mount Uniacke, Lakeland, Nova Scotia
88   17 Edgewater Street, Mahone Bay, Nova Scotia
89   129 Central Street, Chester, Nova Scotia
90   Bloomfield, 2730 Fuller Terrace, Halifax, Nova Scotia
91   Keillor House, 12 Sackville Road, Dorchester, New Brunswick
92   Acacia Grove, Starr's Point, Nova Scotia
93   Admiralty House, Halifax
94   Proposed Elevation for Admiralty House, Halifax
95   Loyalist House, 120 Union Street, Saint John, New Brunswick
96   Crane House, 7 East Main Street, Sackville, New Brunswick
97   18 Fort Lawrence Road, Fort Lawrence, Nova Scotia
98   Kingston, Nova Scotia
99   Dyke Road, Upper Falmouth, Nova Scotia
100 The Ledge, New Brunswick
101 78 King Street, St. Andrews, New Brunswick

46

Legend Sources

1 Rudolph Wittkower, Palladio and Palladianism, p. 75-76.
2 John Summerson, Architecture in Britain, 1530-1830, pp. 192-93.
3 John Harris, op. cit., p. 31-39; John Summerson, Architecture in Britain, 1530-1830, p. 222.
4 Rudolf Wittkower, Architectural Principles, pp. 82-89.
5 James S. Ackerman, op. cit., pp. 68-70.
6 Ibid., p. 58.
12 John Summerson, Architecture in Britain, 1530-1830, pp. 208-9.
14 R.V. Harris, op. cit.
15 Ibid.
16 Heritage Trust of Nova Scotia, St. Mary's Church, Auburn, N.S. 1790 (Halifax: Heritage Trust of Nova Scotia, 1967).
17 Rev. Canon Brigstocke, History of Trinity Church Saint John, New-Brunswick (Saint John, New Brunswick: n.p., 1892); Patrick Campbell, op. cit., p. 21; G. Herbert Lee, An Historical Sketch of the First Fifty Years of the Church of England in the Province of New-Brunswick (1783-1833) (Saint John, New Brunswick: Sun Publ., 1883).
18 David Russell Jack, History of St. Andrews Church, St. John, N.B. (Saint John, New Brunswick: Barnes, 1913).
19 Rev. Archibald Gunn, Sixty-second Anniversary of Greenock Church, St. Andrews, N.B. (Halifax: 1886, n.p.); Grace Helen Mowat, The Diverting History of a Loyalist Town. A Portrait of St. Andrew's, New-Brunswick (Fredericton: Brunswick Press, 1953).
20 William H. Pierson, Jr., op. cit., pp. 137-40.
21 Canada, Public Archives, MG11, C.O. 217, Nova Scotia "A," Vol. 133, pp. 116-19, Sir John Wentworth to the Duke of Portland, 27 July 1801; St. George Church 1800-1975. Halifax, N.S. (N.p.: n.d., n.p.).
22 Quebec. Affaires culturelles, Inventaire des biens culturels, Gérard Morisset Papers, Anglical cathedral file, Quebec; Luc Noppen, Les églises du Québec

(1660-1850), pp. 158-60; F.C. Würtele, op. cit., pp. 76-84.
23 F. Dawson Adams, A History of Christ Church Cathedral, Montreal (Montreal: Burton's, 1941); Lita-Rose Betcherman, "William Von Moll Berczy" (MA thesis, Carleton University, Ottawa, 1962); Florence M. Burns, William Berczy (Don Mills: Fitzhenry and Whiteside, 1977); André Giroux et al., "Inventaire des marchés de construction des Archives nationales du Québec à Montréal, 1800-1830." Manuscript on file, National Historic Parks and Sites Branch, Parks Canada, Ottawa, 1973, Nos 982-88 (now published in History and Archaeology/Histoire et archéologie, 49, 2 vols.); Newton Bosworth, Hochelaga Depicta, or the Early History and Present State of the City and Island of Montreal (Montreal: William Greig, 1839), p. 100-104; H.E. MacDermot, Christ Church Cathedral. A Century in Retrospect (Montreal: The Gazette Printing, 1959); Jean-Claude Marsan, Montréal en évolution (Montreal: Fides, 1974), p. 173-75; Edward Allan Talbot, Voyage au Canada (Paris: Librairie Centrale, 1833), Vol. 1, p. 50-51; Jean Trudel, William Berczy, La famille Woolsey (Ottawa: National Gallery of Canada, 1976).
24 C.P.C. Dounman, ed., A Concise, Chronological and Factual History of St. Stephen's Anglican Church. Chambly, Qué (Montreal: Perry Printing, 1970).
25 P. Galarneau, J. Hallé and D. Lapierre, Comptes rendus de certains bâtiments dans la ville de Montréal (P.Q.) et dans les municipalités avoisinantes, Travail inédit No. 300 (Parks Canada, Ottawa, 1978), p. 147-51; André Giroux et al., op. cit., nos 1531-35; Quebec. Affaires culturelles, Inventaire des biens culturels, Gérard Morisset Papers, Saint-Antoine Church file, Longueuil.
26 Arthur E.E. Legge, The Anglican Church in Three Rivers, Quebec. 1768-1956 (N.p.: n.p., 1956); Luc Noppen, Les églises du Québec 1600-1850, p. 78; John R. Porter and Léopold Désy, op. cit.
27 G. Bastien, D. D. Dubé and C. Southam, "Inventaire des marchés de construction des archives civiles de Québec, 1800-

1870," Histoire et archéologie/History and Archaeology, la (1975), Nos 627-637; Wilfrid F. Butcher, "Two Centuries of Presbyterianism in Old Quebec," The Presbyterian Record, Vol. 84 (May 1959), p. 12; Sir James MacPherson Lemoine, Quebec, Past and Present. A History of Quebec. 1608-1876 (Quebec: A. Côté, 1876), p. 405; Luc Noppen, Les églises du Québec 1600-1850, p. 182; Quebec. Affaires culturelles, Inventaire des biens culturels, Gérard Morisset Papers, St. Andrews Church file, Quebec.

28 P. Galarneau, J. Hallé and D. Lapierre, op. cit., pp. 87-92.

29 Susan Algie, "Reports on Selected Buildings in Ontario." Manuscript on file, National Historic Parks and Sites Branch, Parks Canada, Ottawa, 1979.

30 Canada, Public Archives, RG1, E15A, Board of Audit, Lower Canada, vols. 281-86, Erection of the Quebec Court House, 1799-1804; Line Chabot, Comptes rendus de certains bâtiments dans la ville de Québec (P.Q.) et dans les municipalités avoisinantes, Travail inédit No. 298 (Parks Canada, Ottawa, 1978), p. 19-30; G. Bastien, D. Dubé and C. Southam, op. cit., Nos. 426-32; Lower Canada. House of Assembly, Journal of the House of Assembly of Lower Canada. From the 28th March to the 3rd June 1799 (Quebec: John Neilson, 1799), p. 140-41; Quebec, Affaires culturelles, Inventaire des biens culturels, Gérard Morisset Papers, former court house, Quebec; Quebec. Affaires culturelles, Inventaire des biens culturels, Gérard Morisset Papers, François Baillairgé Journal, 1784-1800, 23 June 1799.

31 Newton Bosworth, op. cit., pp. 158-59; Canada, Public Archives, RG1, E15A, Board of Audit, Lower Canada, Vol. 280, Erection of the Montreal Court House, 1799-1802; André Giroux et al., op. cit., nos. 897-903; Quebec, Affaires culturelles, Inventaire des biens culturels, Gérard Morisset Papers, court house file, Montreal, Jonathan Sewell to William Hall, 2 Sept. 1799.

32 Canada, Public Archives, RG1, E12, Reports and Registers, Vol. 2; RG1, E15A, Board of Audit, Lower Canada, Vol. 290; Newton Bosworth, op. cit.,

33 Luc Noppen, François Baillairgé et son oeuvre, 1759-1830 (Quebec: Musée du Québec, 1975) (hereafter cited as François Baillairgé), p. 75; idem, Dossier d'inventaire architectural de la prison de Trois-Rivières (Quebec: ministère des Affaires culturelles, 1977); Jacques Robert, Les prisons de Trois-Rivières et de Sherbrooke (Quebec: ministère des Affaires culturelles, 1979).

34 Canada, Public Archives, RG1, E15A, Board of Audit, Lower Canada, Vols. 288, 289; Luc Noppen, François Baillairgé, pp. 73-74; Philibert de l'Orme, Premier tome de l'architecture (Paris: Frédéric Morel, 1567), p. 207.

35 Acadian Magazine (Halifax), Vol. 1, No. 3, 3 Sept. 1826, p. 81; Thomas Chandler Haliburton, An Historical and Statistical Account of Nova Scotia (Halifax: Joseph Howe, 1829), Vol. 2, p. 17; Nova Scotia. Provincial Archives, Province House file; John MacGregor, op. cit., p. 140; Hazel M. MacKenzie, "Classical Architecture in Canada. Province House. Halifax. 1811-1819." Term paper, Carleton University, Ottawa, 1978.

36 Christopher William Atkinson, A Historical and Statistical Account of New-Brunswick, B.N.A. with Advice to Emigrants (Edinburgh: Anderson & Bryce, 1844), p. 70; University of New Brunswick, Fredericton, Harriet Irving Library Archives, op. cit.

37 "Old Government House. Woodstock House." Manuscript on file, National Historic Parks and Sites Branch, Parks Canada, Ottawa, n.d.

38 C.A. Hale, The Early Court Houses of New Brunswick, Manuscript Report Series, No. 290 (Ottawa: Parks Canada, 1977), p. 81-91.

39 Mary K. Cullen, A History of the Structure and Use of Province House, Prince Edward Island 1837-1977, Manuscript Report Series No. 211 (Ottawa: Parks Canada, 1977); C.J. Taylor, The Early Court Houses of Prince Edward Island, Manuscript Report Series No. 289 (Ottawa: Parks Canada, 1977), p. 59-65.

40 Shirley B. Elliott, "A History of Province House and Government House," Journal

of Education, Vol. 14, No. 1 (Oct. 1964), p. 42-51; Charles Bruce Ferguson, "Isaac Hildrith (c. 1741-1807) Architect of Government House, Halifax," Dalhousie Review, Vol. 51, No. 4 (winter 1970/1971), p. 510-16; Nova Scotia. Provincial Archives, Government House file.

41 C.J. Taylor, op. cit., pp. 5-6.

42 William Dendy, Lost Toronto (Toronto: Oxford University Press, 1978), p. 37-39.

43 Dana Johnson and Leslie Maitland, "Osgoode Hall," Agenda Paper (1979-50), Historic Sites and Monuments Board of Canada, Ottawa, 1979, pp. 257-72.

44 R. Bill, A. Earle and J. Lewis, Reports on Selected Buildings in St. John's Newfoundland, Manuscript Report Series No. 256 (Ottawa: Parks Canada, 1974), p. 179-90; F.A. O'Dea, "Government House," Canadian Collector, Vol. 10, No. 2 (March/Apr. 1975), p. 48-51.

45 R. Bill, A. Earle and J. Lewis, op. cit., pp. 171-77.

46 Ariane Isler, "Le vieux marché et l'ancienne douane dans le vieux Montréal," Term paper, Department of History, University of Montreal (Jan. 1972). Ariane de Jongh Isler, "L'ancienne douane de Montréal," Vie des Arts, Vol. 20, No. 79 (summer 1975), pp. 39-41; Jean-Claude Marsan, op. cit., pp. 171-71.

47 Anne Hale, "Early Court Houses of Nova Scotia." Manuscript on file, National Historic Parks and Sites Branch, Parks Canada, Ottawa (1979).

48 Newton Bosworth, op. cit., p. 165; André Giroux et al., op. cit., nos. 893-894; Jean-Claude Marsan, op. cit., pp. 169-70; Edward Allen Talbot, Five Years' Residence in the Canadas, Vol. 1, p. 71.

49 Allan Gowans, Building Canada (Toronto: Oxford University Press, 1966), p. 78; Nova Scotia. Provincial Archives, Town Clock file.

50 Joseph Bouchette, Description topographique de la Province du Bas-Canada... (Londres: W. Faden, 1815), p. 467-68; John Lambert, op. cit., Vol. 1, pp. 70-71; Le Courrier de Québec (Quebec), 11 March 1807, pp. 2-3; Canada, Public Archives, National Map Collection, H12/340-Québec-1806, plan for a Quebec market and D340-Québec-

1806, John Bentley report.

51 Mary K. Cullen, "Charlottetown Market Houses 1813-1958," The Island, No. 6 (spring/summer 1979), pp. 27-32.

52 Susan Algie, op. cit., William Dickson House.

53 Eric R. Arthur, Toronto. No Mean City, pp. 16-18.

54 William Dendy, op. cit., p. 15.

55 Roger E. Riendeau, "The Grange." Manuscript on file, National Historic Parks and Sites Branch, Parks Canada, Ottawa, n.d.

56 Idem, "Campbell House." Manuscript on file, National Historic Parks and Sites Branch, Parks Canada, Ottawa, 1974.

57 Dana Johnson and C.J. Taylor, Reports on Selected Buildings in Kingston, Ontario. Manuscript Report Series No. 261 (Ottawa: Parks Canada, 1976-77), pp. 127-31.

59 Marion MacRae, The Ancestral Roof, pp. 11-12. (Toronto, Clarke Irwin, 1963).

60 Ibid., pp. 56-57.

61 Ibid., pp. 41-42.

62 William Dendy, op. cit., pp. 70-77.

63 "Homewood, Maitland, Ontario." Manuscript on file, National Historic Parks and Sites Branch, Parks Canada, Ottawa, n.d.

67 Michael Newton, Maplelawn 1831-1979 (Ottawa: National Capital Commission, 1979).

68 Eric R. Arthur, Toronto, No Mean City, p. 46.

69 Doris Drolet-Dubé and Marthe Lacombe, op. cit., Nos. 842, 843, 1632.

70 Christina Cameron and Jean Trudel, op. cit., pp. 148-49.

71 John R. Porter, Jopseph Légaré 1795-1855. L'Oeuvre, (Ottawa, National Gallery of Canada, 1978), No. 43.

73 P. Galarneau, J. Hallé and D. Lapierre, op. cit., pp. 137-46.

75 Mathilde Brosseau, "Monklands (Villa Maria Convent)," Agenda Paper, May 1974-H, Historic Sites and Monuments Board of Canada, Ottawa, 1974, p. H.6-H.9.

76 Quebec. Affaires culturelles, Inventaire des biens culturels, Sauvageau/Sweeny House file.

77-78 A. C. Buell, Sir William Johnson (New York: Appleton, 1903), pp. 13, 221-22.

79   Raymonde Gauthier, Les Manoirs du Québec (Quebec: Fides, 1976), pp. 27, 80; John G. Waite and Paul R. Huey, Northwest Stonehouse, Johnson Hall a Historic Structure Report (New York: New York State Historic Trust, 1971).

80   P. Galarneau, J. Hallé and D. Lapierre, op. cit., pp. 15-20.

81   G. Bastien, D.D. Dubé and C. Southam, op. cit., No. 440; Raymonde Gauthier, op. cit., p. 172.

82   P. Galarneau, J. Hallé and D. Lapierre, op. cit., pp. 209-25.

83   A.J.H. Richardson, "Guide to the Architecturally and Historically Most Significant Buildings of the Old City of Québec with a Biographical Dictionary of Architects and Builders and Illustrations," Bulletin of the Association for Preservation Technology, Vol. 2, Nos. 3-4 (1970), p. 42.

84   Ibid., pp. 45-46.

85   A.J.H. Richardson, op. cit., pp. 33-34.

86   Nova Scotia. Provincial Archives, Dockyard — Commissioner's House file.

87   Will R. Bird, "Some Historic Houses of Nova Scotia," Canadian Geographical Journal, Vol. 57, No. 2 (Aug. 1952), pp. 62-65.

90   Heritage Trust of Nova Scotia, Founded Upon a Rock, p. 80.

91   "Keillor House Museum, Dorchester, N.B.," brochure (N.p.: n.p.).

92   Nathalie Clerk, "La maison Prescott à Starr's Point." Manuscript on file, National Historic Parks and Sites Branch, Parks Canada, Ottawa, 1980.

93   Anne Hale and Nathalie Clerk, "Admiralty House, CFB Halifax, Halifax, Nova Scotia, Agenda Paper 1978-09, Historic Sites and Monuments Board of Canada, Ottawa, 1978, pp. 108-21.

95   "Loyalist House," brochure (N.p.: n.p.).

1 Queen's House, Greenwich, England

Constructed: 1616–35
Architect: Inigo Jones
Material: stone

The Queen's House embodied the classical precepts of the Italian Renaissance more closely than any building previously constructed in England. In designing it, Jones borrowed several elements from the repertoire of Italian architecture: the rectangular form of the building, the horizontality of the facade as expressed by the delineation of each storey and the use of a rectilinear cornice; the relationships between the openings and the surface of the walls; and the loggia. During his visits to Italy in 1601 and 1613–14 Jones discovered Palladio's works, spoke with Palladio's disciple Scamozzi, and studied and measured the ancient monuments of Rome. In the Queen's House, which he designed not long after returning to England, he applied the new principles he had learned in Italy. This building, like Jones's architectural work as a whole, was not very influential during his lifetime, because he worked exclusively for the court and the aristocracy. His works were rediscovered at the beginning of the eighteenth century, when there was a return to Palladio. (Department of the Environment, Great Britain, with permission of the Controller of Her Majesty's Stationery Office)

2 **Wanstead, Essex, England**

Constructed: 1715-20
Demolished: 1822
Architect: Colen Campbell
Material: stone

According to author John Summerson, the House of Parade was a type of building that adapted the seventeenth century English house to the teachings of Palladio — Wanstead, built in 1715-20 according to a design by Colen Campbell, was a prototype. Composed of a main block flanked by low side wings, the central portion of the building featured a monumental portico consisting of a large pediment supported by six Corinthian columns, which was accessible by two lateral stairways. Side wings completed the composition of the building. In contrast to houses built in the previous century, Wanstead had little ornamentation, and its openings were arranged in an orderly and symmetrical manner. As in the Queen's House, designed by Inigo Jones (Fig. 1), the horizontal character of the building was emphasized by the divisions distinguishing the various storeys and by the cornice. On the other hand, the central portico and the side wings were new features borrowed from the repertoire of Roman architecture. Colen Campbell designed two other plans for this building — one without wings, and the other with wings ending in towers. The building as actually constructed, as well as the two alternative plans, exerted a profound influence on domestic English architecture throughout the eighteenth century. (The British Library, Great Britain)

3 Mereworth, Kent, England

Constructed: 1723
Architect: Colen Campbell
Material: stone

In Palladio's day, the term "villa" designated a rural estate including farm buildings and several houses. The main house in this grouping was known as the "casa di villa." In the eighteenth century, the term "villa" no longer referred to a rural estate, but merely to a country house. For their villas, the Palladians copied certain compact buildings designed by Palladio. Thus, in designing Mereworth, Colen Campbell drew his inspiration from Palladio's Villa Rotonda (Fig. 5). Larger than its model (90 feet square rather than 80), Mereworth was a square, compact building. Contrary to the House of Parade style, which allowed for a variety of adaptations, the English villas as seen here conformed to a fairly standard model: a square plan, a central portico on each side, a raised basement and a facade featuring five openings. In its form, dimensions, composition and ornamentation, Mereworth was one of the prototypes of the English villa. (National Monuments Records, London)

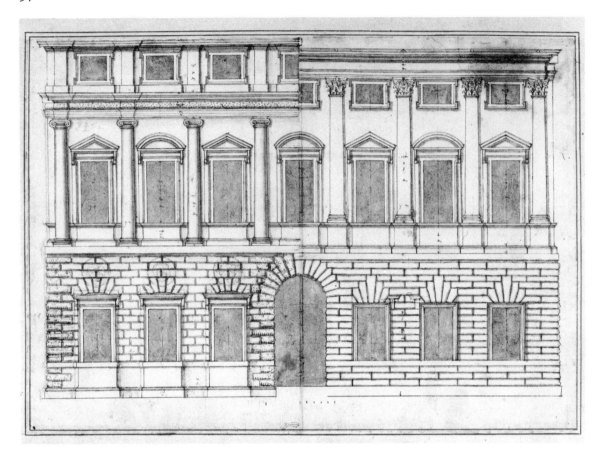

4 Elevation of the Palazzo Porto-Colleoni, Vicenza, Italy

Constructed: ca. 1550
Architect: Andrea Palladio

This elevation of the Palazzo Porto-Colleoni illustrates perfectly a type of composition that became very popular with the eighteenth century Palladians. In designing this building, Palladio drew his inspiration from a group of buildings in Rome designed by Bramante and Raphael. However, he lightened the composi-tion by replacing the double colonnade with a series of simple Ionic columns and by adding certain Venetian motifs, such as masks and festoons, to the final version. For their own designs, the Palladian architects borrowed the main elements of the elevation by Palladio, including the orderly, symmetrical fenestra-tion, the clearly delimited storeys, the raised basement and the absence of superfluous orna-mentation. (The Royal Institute of British Architects, London)

5 Villa Rotonda, Vicenza, Italy

Constructed: 1550-51
Architect: Andrea Palladio
Material: stone

The Villa Rotonda is Palladio's most famous building. It served as a prototype for the English villa. Yet this compact structure, with a porch on each side and a dome on top, is not truly representative, in architectural terms, of what Palladio meant by a villa. Whereas the villas designed by Palladio were usually utilitarian, being located on an agricultural estate, this one is situated near the town, on raised ground, and has no function other than to provide views of the surrounding area, evident in the fenestration and the presence of four porches. (Centro Internazionale di Studi di Architettura "Andrea Palladio")

6 Villa Emo, Fanzolo, Italy

Constructed: ca. 1567
Architect: Andrea Palladio
Material: stone

Italy was undergoing a major economic change during Palladio's day. One aspect of this change was that the aristocracy, until then concerned with trade in the towns and cities, was obliged to move to the rural areas and administer large agricultural holdings. For this wealthy elite, Palladio provided elegant buildings capable of fulfilling various functions under a single roof. The Villa Emo is thoroughly representative of this type of building. It includes a central block with a portico in relief, as well as long lateral wings. Unlike the Villa Rotonda, it is located on an agricultural estate and is partially utilitarian in that its wings are used for agricultural purposes. In the eighteenth century, the English aristocracy also went back to the land; it therefore required buildings designed for this new environment, and turned for inspiration to buildings shown in Palladio's publications, in particular the villas featuring side wings. (Centro Internazionale di Studi di Architettura "Andrea Palladio")

7 Plan and Elevation of a Country House

Proposed: ca. 1750
Architect: Robert Morris

This small country house is characteristic of
an architectural type given wide exposure
through books of models intended for the
middle class. This type of house was to be
highly popular in areas far from London and
especially in the American colonies, because it
was simple in design and easily adaptable. It
nevertheless embodied, in greatly simplified
form, the principles and the most important
characteristics of Palladian domestic architecture. The horizontal division of the facade
is emphasized by the cornice and the course
delineating the basement. The layout and the
form of the openings (small and square on the
top storey, rectangular on the main floor), the
raised basement and the central portico are all
elements associated with Palladianism.
(Robert Morris, *Rural Architecture...*, London,
published by the author, 1750, plate 5. Photo:
The University of British Columbia)

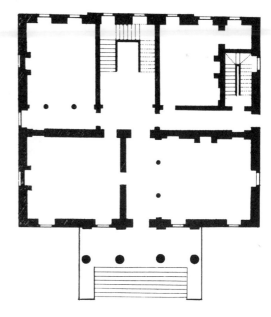

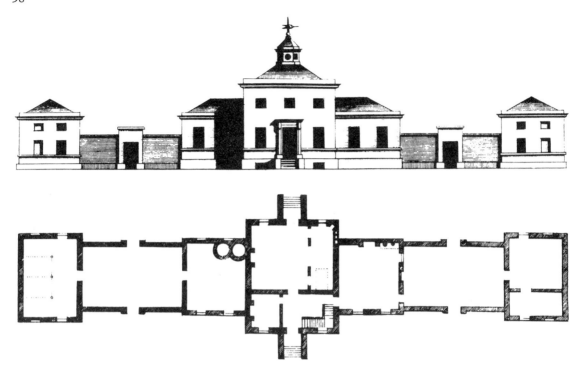

8 **Plan and Elevation of a Country House**

Proposed: ca. 1750
Architect: Robert Morris

This plate, taken from a book of architectural models written by Robert Morris, shows a type of house that colonial builders could easily adapt to suit their needs and imagination. In practice, they often omitted the lateral wings and retained only the central section of the building, usually with its cupola, hipped roof and front door framed by pilasters. In some cases, the builders also copied the wings extending out from the central block, but only rarely did they imitate the pavilions attached by long corridors. (Robert Morris, *Rural Architecture...*, London, published by the author, 1750, plate 3. Photo: The University of British Columbia)

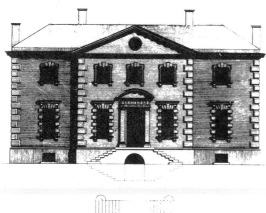

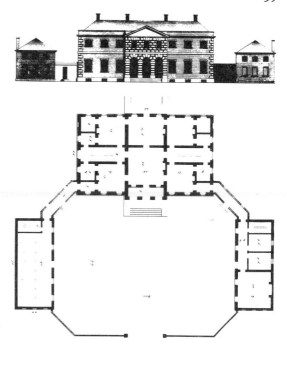

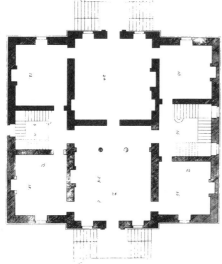

9 Plan and Elevation of a Residence for a Gentleman, Oxfordshire, England

10 Plan and Elevation of a Residence for a Gentleman, Dorsetshire, England

Constructed: eighteenth century
Architect: James Gibbs
This residential design by James Gibbs is typical of the type of composition favoured by colonial builders during the first quarter of the nineteenth century. Because of its simplicity, elegance and adaptability, this architectural type offered numerous advantages for the colonists who adopted this formula of a frontispiece surmounted by a pediment for many of their public buildings, and for some of their homes. The ornamentation used by Gibbs (quoins, keystones over openings, oculus) was also found most frequently on these buildings. (James Gibbs, *A Book of Architecture...*, n.p., W. Innys and R. Manby, 1739, plate 65. Photo: National Gallery of Canada)

Constructed: eighteenth century
Architect: James Gibbs
This residence, located in Dorsetshire, England, is also representative of the buildings proposed by James Gibbs in his *Book of Architecture*. Noteworthy are the projecting frontispiece (which was not always in rusticated stone, however), the course delineating the two storeys, the quoins, the dimensions of the first-storey windows, and the raised basement. Builders in the colonies copied all these motifs in designing public buildings. (James Gibbs, *A Book of Architecture containing Designs of Buildings and Ornaments*, n.p., W. Innys and R. Manby, 1739, plate 58. Photo: National Gallery of Canada)

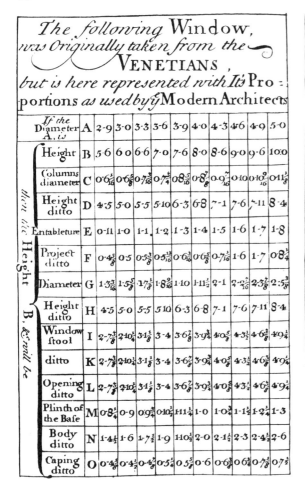

The following Window, was Originally taken from the VENETIANS, but is here represented with Its Proportions as used by ye Modern Architects

If the Diameter A, is	A	2-9	3-0	3-3	3-6	3-9	4-0	4-3	4-6	4-9	5-0
Height	B	5-6	6-0	6-6	7-0	7-6	8-0	8-6	9-0	9-6	10-0
Columns diameter	C	0-6⁴⁄₁₆	0-6⁸⁄₁₆	0-7³⁄₁₆	0-7¹⁄₄	0-8³⁄₁₆	0-8⁵⁄₈	0-9	0-10	0-10⁹⁄₁₆	0-11¹⁄₈
Height ditto	D	4-5	5-0	5-5	5-10	6-3	6-8	7-1	7-6	7-11	8-4
Entableture	E	0-11	1-0	1-1	1-2	1-3	1-4	1-5	1-6	1-7	1-8
Project ditto	F	0-4⁴⁄₈	0-5	0-5³⁄₈	0-5¹³⁄₁₆	0-6³⁄₈	0-6⁵⁄₈	0-7¹⁄₁₆	1-6	1-7	0-8¹⁄₄
Diameter	G	1-3³⁄₁₆	1-5⁵⁄₈	1-7¹⁄₈	1-8¹⁄₄	1-10	1-11¹⁄₂	2-1	2-2²⁄₁₆	2-3³⁄₈	2-5³⁄₄
Height ditto	H	4-5	5-0	5-5	5-10	6-3	6-8	7-1	7-6	7-11	8-4
Window ftool	I	2-7³⁄₈	2-10¹⁄₄	3-1⁸⁄₈	3-4	3-6⁷⁄₈	3-9³⁄₄	4-0⅝	4-3¹⁄₂	4-6³⁄₈	4-9¹⁄₄
ditto	K	2-7³⁄₈	2-10¹⁄₄	3-1⁸⁄₈	3-4	3-6⁷⁄₈	3-9³⁄₄	4-0⅝	4-3¹⁄₂	4-6³⁄₈	4-9¹⁄₄
Opening ditto	L	2-7³⁄₈	2-10¹⁄₄	3-1⁸⁄₈	3-4	3-6⁷⁄₈	3-9³⁄₄	4-0⅝	4-3¹⁄₂	4-6³⁄₈	4-9¹⁄₄
Plinth of the Bafe	M	0-8¹⁄₄	0-9	0-9³⁄₄	0-10¹⁄₂	0-11¹⁄₄	1-0	1-0³⁄₄	1-1¹⁄₂	1-2¹⁄₄	1-3
Body ditto	N	1-4¹⁄₂	1-6	1-7¹⁄₂	1-9	1-10¹⁄₂	2-0	2-1¹⁄₂	2-3	2-4¹⁄₂	2-6
Caping ditto	O	0-4⁴⁄₈	0-4¹⁄₄	0-4³⁄₄	0-5¹⁄₄	0-5³⁄₄	0-6	0-6³⁄₄	0-7³⁄₈	0-7³⁄₄	

then the Height B. &c will be

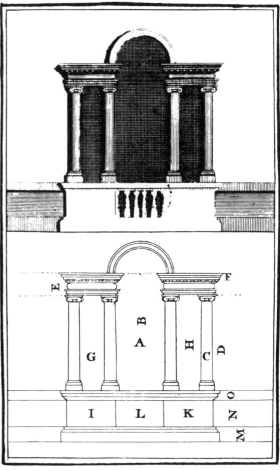

11 **Plate Showing a Venetian Window**

Architect: William Halfpenny

This plate illustrates the type of information provided by the popularizations. These works divided the building into its main parts and provided "recipes" and methods for conforming to the requirements of the most famous architects, including Vitruvius, Palladio and Inigo Jones. It was not unusual to include tables enabling the builder to quickly calculate the dimensions required. In short, these publications provided mainly technical data which small builders and workmen might require. (William Halfpenny, *Practical Architecture...,* London, T. Bowles, 1736, plates 47-48. Photo: Parks Canada)

12 St. Martin-in-the-Fields, London

Constructed: 1721-26
Architect: James Gibbs
Material: stone

During the Palladian period and even afterwards, St. Martin-in-the-Fields in London was the most widely copied and imitated church. Its immense popularity, particularly in the colonies, may be explained by the fact that its plan and elevations were published in the *Book of Architecture* and were therefore easily accessible to builders. Furthermore, in designing this building, Gibbs improved on existing formulas, particularly regarding the steeple and interior layout. The steeple is undeniably the most striking element of the building, as well as the most widely imitated. Having conceived the building as a temple, Gibbs might have been expected to give it merely turrets. Instead, he opted for a steeple arising from within the west wall and emerging through the roof. In so doing, he turned his back not only on the Gothic steeple tradition, but also on the tradition established by his contemporaries, Christopher Wren and Nicholas Hawksmoor, who placed the steeple on the ground, beside the church, or on the west side. On the other hand, the interior layout of St. Martin-in-the-Fields is basically an improved version of a model already developed by Wren: it consists of a rectangular plan, like that of a temple, divided into three parts with side galleries. The exterior treatment of St. Martin-in-the-Fields is much more innovative, especially regarding the imposing portico on the facade. Projecting from the west side of the church, this portico embodies the influence of the Palladian style: it consists of a wide, triangular pediment supported by six Corinthian columns, of which the pilasters adorning the sides of the building are a continuation. One final point: no architectural element on the outside of this building is superfluous, and this in itself is consistent with Palladianism, whose quest for harmony and symmetry was one of the leitmotifs of the movement. (National Monuments Records, London)

The West Front

The Section from South to North

Ja Gibbs Arch del   H Hulsbergh Sculp

13 Marybone Chapel (St. Peter's), Vere Street, London

Constructed: 1721-22
Architect: James Gibbs
Material: brick

The plan and elevations of this chapel, built by James Gibbs for the Earl and Countess of Oxford, are reproduced in the *Book of Architecture*. Gibbs describes the building as follows: "It is a plain Brick Building, except the Portico, Coines, Door-Cases and the Venetian Window...." The building's simplicity, as well as the use of certain motifs derived from a more elaborate style of architecture (Venetian window and portico), explain its popularity in the colonies. In New England it was imitated in several buildings, including the First Baptist Meeting House in Providence, Rhode Island, 1774-75 (Fig. 20). In Canada, it was imitated in wood in St. Paul's Anglican Church in Halifax (Fig. 14). (James Gibbs, *A Book of Architecture containing Designs of Buildings and Ornaments*, n.p., W. Innys and R. Manby, 1739, plate 15. Photo: National Gallery of Canada)

14 **St. Paul's Anglican Church, Halifax**

A plan of the town of Halifax drawn up by Moses Harris in 1749 shows the sites proposed at that time for Government House, the court house and the church. By September 1750 the church was completed. It was, however, situated opposite the site originally proposed on the military parade grounds. The building was constructed quickly to emphasize the British and Anglican presence on the military base. The builders used the best technology available, as well as a prestigious model: "The frame of the church will be here next month from New England, the plan is the same with that of Marybone Chapel." This engraving by Richard Short, dating from 1759, shows St. Paul's before the alterations it underwent in 1812. Originally it was a rectangular building which did indeed resemble James Gibbs's Marybone Chapel in the organization of the rear facade, the form and position of the steeple, the type of openings and the quoins. Short's engraving reveals that originally the south side of the building was also used as an entrance. (Public Archives Canada, C 4293)

15 St. Paul's Anglican Church, 1 St. Paul's Hill, Halifax

Constructed: 1750
Alterations: 1812, 1860–70
Material: wood

During the nineteenth century, this church underwent various alterations that eliminated the similarities between it and Marybone Chapel and disrupted the original arrangement of its openings and its proportions. In 1812 the steeple was so deteriorated that it was deemed necessary to reconstruct it (on the model of the original). Also at this time the building was lengthened by fifteen feet on its north side by adding a vestibule. The aisles and sanctuary were added and the original windows (including the Venetian window on the south side) were altered during 1860–70. (Canadian Inventory of Historic Building)

16 St. Mary's Anglican Church, Auburn, Nova Scotia

Constructed: 1790 by William Matthews
Material: wood

St. Mary's Anglican Church in Auburn was formerly known as St. Mary of Aylesford. It is located in the Annapolis Valley, which began to be settled in 1755 by immigrants from New England. Construction began in 1790, and the church was consecrated on October 10, 1790 by the bishop of Nova Scotia, Charles Inglis, who wrote that it was "the neatest and best finished church in the province...and would be an ornament to any village in England." Tradition has it that William Matthews was the builder. One of Aylesford's major landowners, James Morden, donated six acres of land for the church, on condition that a pew in it be reserved for his family. Moreover, one of the reasons for constructing the church was to accommodate his farmers and attract new settlers. The facade of this church features a triangular pediment more steeply sloped than allowed by classical architecture standards and a bell tower partially placed in front of the facade, as in certain churches of Christopher Wren. By contrast, the pilasters and the pediment adorning the main entrance, and the keystones adorning the windows and the pilasters surrounding them, are evidence of the influence of James Gibbs. This church thus illustrates very well how certain motifs borrowed from classical architecture can be incorporated into a small building. The addition of these elements (especially the pilasters and pediments) gives this church an air of monumentality that is unusual in buildings of this type. (Canadian Inventory of Historic Building)

17 **Trinity Anglican Church, Germain Street, Saint John, New Brunswick**

Constructed: 1788-91
Partially demolished: 1849
Material: wood

Construction of this church, which stood on the east side of Germain Street between Duke and Queen streets in Saint John, N.B., began in 1788 and continued until 1791. The tower and cupola crowning the building were not constructed until 1809-10. As early as 1812 it was proposed that the building be enlarged. Part of the church burned in 1849. In its massive, rectangular form, this church resembles a house. The front and side openings, with round arches featuring keystones, as well as the arrangement and ornamentation of the facade, denote the Palladian influence. The facade also features a wide, triangular pediment enclosing a semicircular opening, pilasters at either end of the wall, a central door given prominence by a small portico surmounted by a pediment, and two side doors with rectangular transoms above. Only the steeple, added later, is heavy and compact and out of character with this facade. This wooden church had a somewhat monumental appearance owing to an ingenious artifice that the English traveller Patrick Campbell noted during a visit to Saint John: the church, he wrote, was "so well painted on the outside that without a strict examination, any spectator would conclude it to be built of stone and lime." (The New Brunswick Museum)

18 St. Andrew's Presbyterian Church, Germain Street, Saint John, New Brunswick

Constructed: 1814-15
Demolished: 1877
Material: wood

It was in 1814 that Saint John's Presbyterian community, which had founded the town in 1783, began taking steps toward building a church. The time was ripe for the construction of such buildings in Saint John, for another house of worship, St. Malachi's Catholic Church, was built there the following year. After the purchase of a lot on Germain Street measuring 100 by 200 feet, calls for tender were posted for the construction of a "scotch church 80 feet long, 50 feet wide, 30

feet posts and 15 feet rise of roof...the sills to be of Norway pine and the sleepers of white pine and the rest of the lumber spruce." The church was completed in 1815. Its facade featured several characteristically Palladian elements such as the wide triangular pediment, supported in this instance by engaged columns; the round-arched windows decorated with keystones; and the three doors surmounted by pediments. The steeple, consisting of a square base and a tall spire, was not elaborate, but it bore a closer resemblance to the steeples of the great Palladian churches than the one of Trinity Anglican Church, also in Saint John (Fig. 17). (The New Brunswick Museum)

19 Greenock Presbyterian Church, St. Andrews, New Brunswick

Constructed: 1821-24
Material: wood

Construction of this church began about 1821, instigated by Reverend John Cassilis, pastor for the Presbyterian community in St. Andrews. Work was halted for a time, then resumed about 1824 owing to the initiative of a Scottish merchant named Christopher Scott, who is said to have had plans sent from Scotland in order to finish construction. The church illustrates the final stage in the evolution of the meeting house, a building type introduced into Canada by the Loyalists. The rectangular body of the building is indeed that of a meeting house, but its facade features a steeple and a projecting frontispiece. It is this steeple, standing out from the facade, which marks the end of the distinctions that until then existed between the meeting house and the traditional church. The steeple is doubly interesting in that its position on the front of the building perpetuates the tradition of Christopher Wren, while its design recalls the works of James Gibbs. In its use of wood and its classical ornamentation applied to a structure characteristic of a meeting house, this church resembles certain houses of worship in New England, such as the First Baptist Meeting House in Providence (Fig. 20). (Public Archives Canada, PA 20684)

20 First Baptist Meeting House, Providence, Rhode Island

Constructed: 1774-75 by Joseph Brown
Material: wood

According to American author William H. Pierson, Jr., the First Baptist Meeting House is the most significant religious building constructed in New England in the years preceding the American Revolution. Designed by Joseph Brown, a well-to-do afficionado of architecture who possessed a copy of James Gibbs's *Book of Architecture*, the building reflects the double influence of New England architecture and Palladianism. Its originally square design and its clapboard siding are typical of the New England architectural tradition of the meeting house. The influence of certain illustrations from the *Book of Architecture* is particularly evident in the composition of the steeple and the portico. The steeple contrasts particularly with the austerity of the rest of the building. With its tall spire and its distinctly differentiated sections, it recalls some of Gibbs's works. The portico too, with its small pediment and Doric columns, shows the influence of Gibbs. (The Rhode Island Historical Society)

21 St. George's Anglican Church, Brunswick Street, Halifax

Constructed: 1800-1801
Alterations: nineteenth century
Architect: William Hughes
Material: wood

On July 27, 1801 the lieutenant-governor of Nova Scotia, John Wentworth, wrote to the secretary of state, the Duke of Portland, to inform him of the opening of St. George's Church: "... St-George Chapel in Halifax, toward the building of which His Majesty was graciously pleased to grant two hundred pounds, is now so far completed, as to be opened for public worship on sunday the 19th instant...." This church replaced an earlier one known as the "Old Dutch Church," which had been constructed about 1753 to serve Halifax's German community but which had soon become too small, especially after the arrival of the Loyalist immigrants. Undoubtedly the most striking feature of St. George's Anglican Church is its circular form. This design, unique in the colony, expresses an architectural concept of Palladio according to which the circle is the ideal form for temples, both for technical and for philosophical reasons. Although the English Palladian architects adhered to this idea in principle, they seldom applied it. It is therefore surprising to find such a building in the colony. Several authors attribute responsibility for it to the Duke of Kent. William Hughes is generally considered to be the building's architect; but the names of J.F. Desbarres and John Merrick are also sometimes mentioned. Several major changes have been made to the building since its construction: the sanctuary was added in 1827, and the additions to the east and west sides also date from the 1820s. The upper gallery was lengthened in 1841. A new entrance was constructed in 1911, and a Venetian window located on the west side was eliminated at that time. Despite these changes, the building still retains its original circular character. (Heritage Recording Services, Parks Canada)

22 Holy Trinity Anglican Cathedral, 31 Desjardins Street, Quebec City

Constructed: 1800-1804
Architects: Captain William Hall and Major William Robe
Material: stone

After the conquest, the Récollets allowed Quebec City's Protestant community to use their chapel for religious services, but the chapel soon proved to be too small. Two events took place that favoured the construction of a new building of more imposing dimensions: in 1793, the Anglican Diocese of Quebec City was founded, necessitating the construction of a cathedral; and three years later, the chapel of the Récollets burned down. Built in less than four years on the former site of the chapel of the Récollets, Holy Trinity Anglican Cathedral was consecrated in August 1804 by the first Anglican bishop of Quebec City, Reverend Jacob Mountain. It was the first Anglican cathedral built outside the British Isles and was designed by Captain William Hall of the Royal Artillery and Major William Robe, an officer in the garrison. According to Robe, the dimensions of the building were taken from St. Martin-in-the-Fields, and the main sources of inspiration for the compositional elements and the proportions were the works of Palladio, Alberti and Vitruvius. Owing to the limited availability of materials, the level of experience of local workmen and climatic conditions, it was necessary to simplify the proportions and spatial relationships originally planned. The pilasters on the facades projected less than Palladio's rules prescribed, because the stone from Pointe-aux-Trembles could not be quarried in very sizable blocks, and in 1818 the pitch of the roof was increased to adapt to the harsh conditions of winter. Instead of the portico composed of a pediment and six Corinthian columns which adorned the facade of St. Martin's, Holy Trinity was given a wide pediment supported by pilasters and an arcade. The steeple of Holy Trinity was less ornate and refined than that of Gibbs, but it had the same basic design consisting of a square base composed of successively smaller sections, terminating in a tall spire. The rectangular design of the building and the division of the interior space into three naves and side gal-

leries were borrowed directly from St. Martin's. This building was to be particularly influential in the Quebec City area. The steeple with its four parts of successively diminishing size and its square base; the facade adorned with pilasters, an arcade and a wide triangular pediment enclosing an oculus; the Venetian window in back; and the interior layout reflected in the three entrances were all innovations that were copied and adopted in modified form in the small churches of various denominations. (Heritage Recording Services, Parks Canada)

23 Christ Church Anglican Cathedral, Montreal

Constructed: 1805-20
Demolished: 1856
Architect: William Berczy
Material: stone

Constructed under the supervision of William Gilmore, this church opened for services in 1814, although the steeple was not built until 1819-20. The most striking features of the facade are the Doric pediment supported by pilasters of the Tuscan order, the cornice, the rectangular windows with keystones and consoles, and the steeple. Gibbs's influence is particularly evident in the cornice, the type of openings, the quoins at either end, and the steeple. The steeple, like its counterpart at St. Martin-in-the-Fields, is placed behind the pediment and the cornice. It stands on a square base and consists of a drum with a round-headed window, terminating in a tall spire. The church was designed by William Berczy, probably during a visit to Montreal in 1804. Berczy is thought to have received architectural training at the Academy of Vienna during the 1750s. He travelled in the United States and Europe, where he was able to observe new architectural trends: he was in Italy at the end of the 1770s; in London in 1790-99; and in Newport (Rhode Island), New York and Philadelphia from 1792 to 1794. His knowledge of architecture, gained in study and in travel abroad, is reflected in the design of the facade of Christ Church Cathedral, where Palladian elements are combined with certain Neoclassical motifs, such as recessed panels and the volute over the door. (Université de Montréal, Centrale de photographie, J. Recasens)

24 St. Stephen's Anglican Church, Chambly, Quebec

Constructed: 1820-22
Material: stone

Plans to build a church for the Protestant population of Chambly date from 1817; actual construction began in 1820. The design was probably developed by Reverend Edward Parkin, pastor of the parish from 1819 to 1828. The construction was carried out by François Valade. This church is interesting because it combines elements of traditional Quebec architecture with certain Palladian motifs. In the simplicity of its plan (rectangular, with a semicircular apse at the far end) and its masonry of rough, unhewn stone, it belongs to the architectural tradition of Quebec. To this rather simple structure is added a Venetian window in the apse, as well as a false pediment and a semicircular window on the facade. The builder's contract specifies that the main door must be of freestone, with a transom above, and that the wooden portal is to be of the Tuscan order. The interior layout (with galleries on the upper floor) is modelled on that of Anglican churches. (Heritage Recording Services, Parks Canada)

25 St. Antoine Catholic Church, Longueuil, Quebec

Constructed: 1810-13
Demolished: 1884
Architect: Pierre Conefroy
Material: stone

This stone church, measuring 126 by 51 feet with two protruding chapels, was built according to the plans and specifications of Abbé Pierre Conefroy, vicar-general for the Montreal area and priest of the Boucherville parish, who already had several other churches to his credit, including the one in Boucherville (1802). The Longueuil church was built according to a format standardized by Conefroy: a plan in the form of a Latin cross with an apse at the far end. The facade of the building is particularly interesting, because it employs — with a much more grandiose effect — the layout and some of the motifs of the Boucherville church, including the centre door with its Ionic order surmounted by a pediment, the two side doors topped by cornices, the two round windows superimposed, and the round-arched windows above the side doors. The facade also features new motifs, such as the wide triangular pediment, the small, triangular blind windows and the pilasters supporting the small pediment. These decorative motifs illustrate the integration of the Palladian style into the architecture of Quebec's parish churches. (Inventaire des biens culturels du Québec)

26 St. James Anglican Church, Trois-Rivières

Constructed: 1754
Alterations: 1796, 1823
Material: stone

This church was occupied by the Récollets until the last member of this order departed in 1776 and subsequently it was used by the Anglican community who made certain alterations to the church in 1796. In 1823 consideration was given to selling the church in order to construct a new one in a more appropriate location. However, it was decided to alter the existing building: a new roof was to be added, with a cornice projecting eighteen inches; a new tower and a spire were to be built; and the outside walls were to be roughcast. The interior alterations were designed primarily to renovate the furnishings (the pulpit, altar and lecterns) and redevelop the space inside the building. This work was performed by Joseph Clark and Terry Appleton, who in 1819-20 had together been responsible for joinery work on the steeple of the Anglican cathedral of Montreal (Fig. 23). These alterations made the building more suitable for Anglican services. They also illustrated the Palladian influence on existing, traditional-type buildings. The slope of the roof was increased, and the facade was ornamented with a wide pediment featuring a round window, typical of the great Palladian churches. (Heritage Recording Services, Parks Canada)

27 St. Andrew's Presbyterian Church, 106 Ste-Anne Street, Quebec City

Constructed: 1809-10 by John Bryson
Alterations: 1823-24
Material: stone

Following the arrival of the American Loyalists, it became necessary to build a church in Quebec City to accommodate the Presbyterian community which since the conquest had been gathering to worship at the College of the Jesuits. The government granted land for this purpose in 1808. Construction began in July 1809 and was completed in 1810 under the supervision of John Bryson, who had worked as a joiner in the construction of the city's Anglican cathedral (Fig. 22). The church was expanded in 1823-24 and John Phillips was put in charge of masonry. The new steeple, constructed by Jean-Baptiste Caillouet, was modelled on that of the Anglican cathedral. Like the latter, it had a square base and consisted of five sections of diminishing size. Following these alterations, the building featured several new, Palladian-inspired elements, such as the triangular pediment and the semicircular openings (shown in an engraving dating from 1829). (Heritage Recording Services, Parks Canada)

28 St. Gabriel's Presbyterian Church, Champ de Mars, Montreal

Constructed: 1792
Demolished: 1903
Material: stone

On April 2, 1792 the members of Montreal's Scottish Presbyterian congregation acquired a lot on St. Gabriel Street (then known as St. Phillipe Street) to build that same year a church measuring 60 by 48 feet, designed to accommodate 650 people. In 1806 additional carpentry was carried out, and in 1809 the steeple was constructed, along with a new roof. The church was used for services until it was sold in 1886; it was demolished in 1903. This church illustrates how the new architectural style could affect small religious buildings. It exhibits some of the more striking features of the monumental churches, such as the wide pediment (which in this case is out of scale with the rest of the facade) enclosing a round window, the keystones above the windows, and the quoins around the door and at either end of the front wall. The little steeple stands on a square base and ends in a spire. The facade has been made higher than the rest of the building, probably to create a more grandiose effect. In its form, proportions and rather austere ornamentation, this first Protestant church built in Montreal is not unlike certain small parish churches in Scotland. (Public Archives Canada, PA 22193)

29 St. Andrew's Presbyterian Church, Williamstown, Ontario

Constructed: 1812-18
Material: stone

The establishment of a Presbyterian congregation in Upper Canada coincided with the arrival of a first group of Loyalists in Williamstown in 1787, under the leadership of Sir John Johnson. That same year, a first church, made of logs, was built. A second church, constructed in 1810, collapsed not long after it was built. The construction of the existing St. Andrews Church began in 1812 and was completed in 1818. The building's fieldstone construction and its squat shape, characteristic of traditional Quebec architecture, are rather elegantly blended with Palladian architectural elements, as seen in the type of openings and their arrangement on the facade, as well as the position of the steeple on the roof. This use of the classical vocabulary gives the building a much more refined appearance. Elements peculiar to the architecture of Quebec on this Ontarian church may be explained by the fact that two contractors from Quebec participated in its construction: the walls, built in 1812, were the work of François-Xavier Rocheleau, a Quebec City mason who had settled in Kingston, and the steeple (1816) was built by Pierre Poitras of Montreal. In this part of Ontario there were several other buildings (especially houses) constructed by builders from Lower Canada, and this may explain the blend of architectural traditions (Quebec-based, Loyalist and English) found in this area before 1812 (for example, Fig. 63). (Canadian Inventory of Historic Building)

30 Court House, St. Louis Street, Quebec City

Constructed: 1799-1803
Burned down: 1873
Material: stone

Located just south of the Anglican cathedral on the corner of St. Louis Street and Place d'Armes, on the site of the existing court house, this building stood on land that since 1681 had belonged to the Récollets and that the government had acquired after this order's church and convent burned down on September 6, 1796. Construction of the building began in 1799 and continued until 1803. Captain William Hall, who may have assisted in designing the building, was responsible for overseeing its construction. Over the years, various repairs were made to it. We know in particular that a cupola was placed on the roof in 1839 and that a wing was added in 1853. The building burned down in 1873. The identity of the architect of this building has not been clearly established, but François Baillairgé is known to have submitted a plan for the ground floor and the upper storey on June 23, 1799. In September 1799 Jonathan Sewell, one of the three commissioners overseeing the work, wrote to Captain Hall to discuss the plan. This letter indicates that Sewell consulted various architectural treatises for a plan. Could he have drawn upon certain models presented in Gibbs's *Book of Architecture* (plates LVII, LVIII) which offer similarities with the building (Fig. 10)? The letter also indicates Sewell ascribed particular importance to the portico and the interior layout of the building. We may therefore assume that Sewell and Hall altered the original plans by Baillairgé, or that they simply drew up new ones. This court house is one of the first public buildings constructed in the colony by the new government. With its rectangular form and its projecting frontispiece, it is typical of the buildings inspired by Gibbs's form of Palladianism. This frontispiece is surmounted by a pediment formed by the cornice of the roof. Originally this was to be a wooden cornice, but instead it was decided to construct a cornice "in stone of the tuscan order...on account of its propriety, its durability, its safety from fire and its superior degree of ornament." The quoins at the corners of the walls, the stone course demarcating the storeys from one another, the form of the roof and the round-headed doors are other elements reflecting Gibbs's influence. (Public Archives Canada, PA 51756)

31 **Court House, Notre-Dame Street, Montreal**

Constructed: 1799–1803 by François-Xavier Daveluy
Demolished: 1844
Material: stone

The construction of this building began in October 1799 and ended in 1803. François-Xavier Daveluy was the builder and William Gilmore the overseer of construction. Built at the same time as its counterpart in Quebec City, this court house uses the same formula of a central frontispiece and is also a two-storey rectangular building ornamented with a course and quoins. However, the use of diverse and plentiful decoration gives this building a more refined appearance, for example, the emblem and an urn on the pediment, modillions on the cornice, arcades around the central windows, and Venetian windows at the ends of the building. There was a certain rivalry between the cities of Quebec and Montreal, and the ornamentation used on the Montreal building is perhaps a manifestation of this. (Public Archives Canada, C 13342)

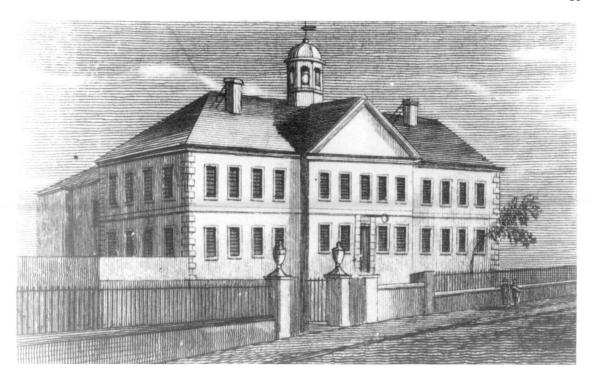

32 **Prison, Notre-Dame Street, Montreal**

Constructed: 1808-1809 (demolished)
Material: stone

This building was constructed in 1808-1809 near the court house, on the site of the original prison which had burned down five years earlier. Louis Charland prepared the plans and specifications for it, under the direction of two of the three commissioners, Pierre-Louis Panet and Joseph Frobisher. There was a dispute between the latter two and a third commissioner, Louis Ogden, concerning the design of the building. Ogden proposed an alternative design (for a windowless building at a higher cost). Panet and Frobisher defended their plan, arguing it was more in keeping with the recommendations of the Englishman John Howard, who since the third quarter of the eighteenth century had been advocating prison reform. Their plan was

ultimately accepted, with several modifications. The masonry work was carried out first by Joseph Morin and then by François-Xavier Daveluy dit Larose. Antoine Bouthilier did the carpentry and joinery. The work was supervised first by William Gilmore and then by Louis Charland. The construction contracts show that this two-storey building measuring 150 by 50 feet was to be of rock-faced stone up to the first plinth, and of picked stone above this level, in the absence of cut stone. Whereas the adjacent building, the court house, featured varied and plentiful ornamentation, the prison appeared very sober as the only decorative touches were the quoins, the stone course demarcating the storeys, and the cupola adorning the roof. (Public Archives Canada, C 13342)

33 Prison, 842 des Prisons Street, Trois-Rivières

Constructed: 1816-19
Architect: François Baillairgé
Material: stone

Like the prison and court house in Montreal and the court house in Quebec City, the Trois-Rivières prison is a rectangular building with a central frontispiece surmounted by a pediment. Like the Montreal prison, its decorative treatment is limited: the pediment contains a round window, quoins accentuate the corners, and courses are used to demarcate the storeys. Originally there was a cupola on the roof. Although it is consistent with the tradition of administrative buildings constructed in Montreal and Quebec City at the beginning of the nineteenth century, this prison differs in its dimensions. It has three storeys, and the three openings in each section of the facade create a rhythm absent in other buildings of this type. The plans and specifications for this building were drawn up by François Baillairgé in 1815. Construction began in 1816 and was essentially completed in 1819, although work continued until 1822. Olivier LaRue was responsible for masonry, and Michel Robitaille for carpentry and joinery. (Canadian Inventory of Historic Building)

34 Prison (now Morrin College), 44 St. Stanislas Street, Quebec City

Constructed: 1808-11
Architect: François Baillairgé
Material: stone

François Baillairgé designed this prison and supervised its construction. In it he made highly original use of the formula of a rectangular block with frontispiece. The frontispiece projects from the facade considerably and is accentuated by its ornamentation. The design is based on a mathematical formula of seven units, put forward by French architect Philibert de L'Orme (1500-1570). According to Baillairgé himself, the compositional pattern is broken because the pilasters and the cornice on the side sections were eliminated by the commissioners overseeing the project. Although this prison is similar in its basic design to other early nineteenth century administrative buildings in Quebec, it is set apart by the use of techniques associated with classical French architecture, visible in the rhythm that Baillairgé wanted to give his facade and in the elegant, sophisticated ornamentation he applied to it. As Luc Noppen has pointed out, this Doric ornamentation is interesting because it subtly integrates the windows of the top storey with the metopes and triglyphs. (Canadian Inventory of Historic Building)

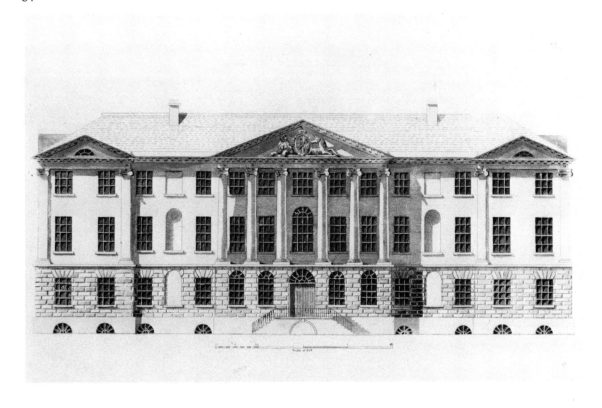

35 Elevation of Province House, 1600 Hollis Street, Halifax

Constructed: 1811-18
Material: stone

As early as 1798 there were plans to construct a building in Halifax to house the legislature, the courts and the public administration, but it was not until 1811 that work actually began. One reason for this long delay was the construction of the Governor's House, which extended from 1800 to 1807 (Fig. 40). John Merrick is generally thought to have drawn up the plans for the legislative building, but *Acadian Magazine* (1826) mentions Richard Scott in this regard. In any event, whoever designed the building had a good knowledge of architecture. This building represents the best use of a Palladian compositional formula found in Canada. The main floor of rusticated stone supports the columns located on the upper storeys. In the central portion of the building, six Ionic columns support a wide triangular pediment featuring an emblem. Some windows are semicircular, and the centre door has a semicircular transom. In the side sections, there are small pediments supported by pilasters. The regular spacing of the openings and the manner in which their dimensions vary (those on the top storey are smaller) are another expression of Palladian principles. The sides of the building also feature pilasters supporting a small central pediment which frames a Venetian window. The arrangement of decorative motifs, openings, pilasters and columns shows in a highly unusual manner a concern for harmony and symmetry typical of the great Palladian buildings in England. Indeed, the building aroused several favourable comments during the nineteenth century, such as those of MacGregor (1828) and Haliburton (1829). (Public Archives Canada, C 3560)

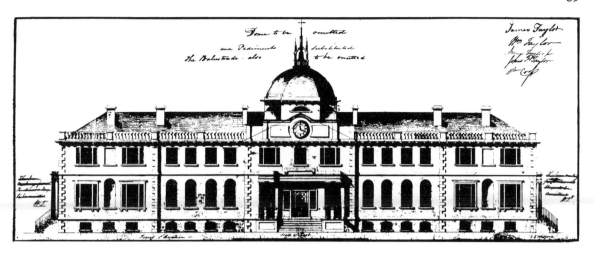

36 Elevation of the Arts Building, University of New Brunswick, Fredericton

Constructed: 1826-27
Alterations: 1876
Architect: John Elliott Woolford
Material: stone

In 1826 the committee responsible for the construction of this building, headed by W. Odell, accepted the plan submitted by John Elliott Woolford. However, for financial reasons, this plan was altered. Woolford had proposed a dome to crown the central part of the roof; it was replaced by a less costly central pediment. The roof, originally to be of tin, was instead made of slate. An ornamental balustrade was to have run along the cornice; this too was omitted. Despite these changes to the original plan, the building nevertheless has an elaborate appearance. It consists of a two-storey rectangular block, with a projecting frontispiece at its centre surmounted by a pediment. Its most distinctive features are the projection of the ends of the facade and the treatment of the main door, which is framed by a semicircular transom on top and small windows on either side. Some twenty years after its completion, it was described as "...The principal building in Fredericton, and perhaps the finest architectural structure in the Province, is the University of King's College, which occupies a commanding position on the hill in rear the town...." In 1876 a third storey was added to the building, and in keeping with the style of the day, it was covered with a mansard roof. (Harriet Irving Library, University of New Brunswick)

37   RCMP Headquarters (formerly Government House), 20 Woodstock Road, Fredericton

Constructed: 1826-28
Architect: John Elliott Woolford
Material: stone

The first Government House in Fredericton (1787) was a modest wooden building constructed by Cornelius Ackerman and Abraham Vanderbeck. After this building burned down in 1825, Sir Howard Douglas, lieutenant-governor of New Brunswick, ordered that a replacement be built. Construction, possibly based on the plans of John Elliott Woolford, began that same year, and the new residence was completed in July 1828. It was a rectangular, three-storey building, the design of which was inspired by Palladian domestic architecture. The facade featured a frontispiece surmounted by a pediment. The form and regular spacing of the openings also reflected the Palladian influence. By contrast, the circular portico and the adjacent sections of the building were Neoclassical inspired. (Canadian Inventory of Historic Building)

38 Court House *(left foreground)*, **20 Sydney Street, Saint John, New Brunswick**

Constructed: 1826-29
Architect: John Cunningham
Material: stone

Before this building was constructed, the court in Saint John held its sessions in a modest wooden building on Germain Street. In about 1797, the court moved to the top floor of the town hall in Market Square. In 1823 the authorities invited submissions for a more appropriate building, and in 1824 John Cunningham's design was selected. It was actually an adaptation of the design submitted by another applicant, Thomas Rust. Construction began in 1826 and continued until 1830, although the building opened for use in 1829. It was the only stone court house in New Brunswick before 1900. It was, however, in conformity with other administrative buildings constructed in the Atlantic region during 1815-30. Its facade features a rusticated ground floor and a frontispiece surmounted by a pediment. Various ornamental elements heighten the elegant appearance of the building: the Doric pilasters supporting the pediment, the stringcourse demarcating the ground floor, and the pilasters framing the ends of the building. There are also several Neoclassical elements, such as the arcades surrounding the windows. Following the fire of February 1919, there were various exterior renovations (beginning in 1924): the roof was covered with copper, the chimneys were moved and a small lantern was placed at the top of the pediment. (Public Archives Canada, C 80165)

39 Province House, 165 Richmond Street, Charlottetown

Constructed: 1843-48
Architect: Isaac Smith
Material: stone

Despite its relatively late construction, the design of Province House draws on a device made popular by the Palladian style. Contrary to earlier buildings, which often featured a central pediment on their facade, this building has a wide portico consisting of four columns supporting a pediment. The use of this portico marks the final stage in the evolution of this Palladian-inspired formula. On the earlier buildings, the ground floor provided a backing for pilasters supporting a pediment, whereas here it is a base for columns performing a similar function. Here again, the main elements of the design converge on the central vertical axis of the building. The recessed ends of the facade are a novelty in terms of the rules established by the Palladians and further enliven the facade. (Canadian Inventory of Historic Building)

40 Governor's House, 1451 Barrington Street, Halifax

Constructed: 1800-1807
Architect: Isaac Hildrith
Material: stone

From the time of his arrival in 1792, the new governor of Nova Scotia, Sir John Wentworth, pressed for a residence that reflected the importance of his position. Seven years later, the government authorized the expenditure of £10,500 to purchase land and construct a new residence. The lot located south of Hollis Street was the one chosen originally for Province House (Fig. 35). Work began in 1800 and was completed in 1807. The cost of the building had risen to three times the amount originally allotted. A comment made in 1808 by Sir George Prevost, Wentworth's successor, confirms that the undertaking had gotten out of hand: the building, he said, was "an edifice out of all proportion to the situation and the cause of my predecessor's reduced circumstances." This official residence was indeed elegant. Its design was Palladian inspired: the ground floor was rusticated, the east side of the facade featured pilasters, the windows on the top storey were small and square, the main door was (originally) surmounted by a semicircular transom and sheltered by a small portico. On the other facade were Neoclassical motifs such as recessed panels, arcades and side wings ending in hemicycles. What is today the front facade was originally the rear. Isaac Hildrith is generally considered to be the architect of this building; he also supervised its construction. (Heritage Recording Services, Parks Canada)

41 **Elevation of Court House, Queen Square, Charlottetown**

Constructed: 1811
Demolished: 1972
Architect: John Plaw
Material: wood

This building, Prince Edward Island's first court house, was constructed in 1811 according to a plan prepared in 1810 by English architect John Plaw. It was originally located on Queen Square (the present-day Confederation Centre) but was moved in 1873 to a site on Euston Street, where it was demolished in 1972. A wooden building approximately 55 by 35 feet, it consisted of a central block flanked by small side wings. The ornamentation for the main door (pediment, pilasters and transom) gave this small building a proud appearance. (Public Archives of Prince Edward Island)

42 Upper Canada College, King Street West, Toronto

Constructed: 1829-31
Demolished: 1900
Architect: J.G. Chewett
Material: brick

Soon after the establishment of Upper Canada College (1829) by a royal charter issued by George IV, construction began on this building according to plans prepared by J.G. Chewett. With its central block flanked by lateral wings,
it is Palladian inspired. The central block is the most important element of the design; it is particularly accentuated by its proportions, its central portico and certain decorative motifs such as the architraves over the windows. The lateral wings, slighty set back, appear more austere. The building underwent major alterations during 1876-77; it was abandoned in 1891 and demolished in 1900. (Public Archives Canada, C 1668)

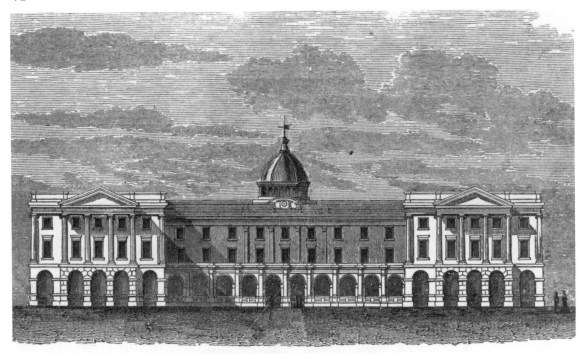

43 Osgoode Hall, 140 Queen Street East, Toronto

Constructed: 1829, 1844-46
Alterations: 1857 and nineteenth century
Material: brick

Constructed in 1829, this building was enlarged in 1844-46 by architect Henry Bower Lane. It then became a long, rectangular, three-storey building with a cupola on top and projecting side sections. Like several other public buildings erected in this country — in some cases fairly late in the nineteenth century — Osgoode Hall embodies some of the major design principles advanced by the Palladians. Particularly noteworthy is the regular spacing and form of the openings, as well as the division of the facade into three distinct horizontal sections (ground floor, second and third floors). In the side sections, the ground floor serves as an anchor for columns supporting a central pediment. Also in evidence are certain Neoclassical motifs, such as the high cornice and the parapet which disguise the angle of the roof. This practice of introducing Neoclassical elements into a Palladian design became popular in the 1820s. The alterations made to this building in later years, moveover, accentuated its Neoclassical character. (Public Archives Canada, C 3261)

44   Government House, 80 Military Road, St. John's, Newfoundland

Constructed: 1827-31
Architect: Thomas Cochrane
Material: stone

This solid stone building, composed of a central block flanked by side wings, has a most interesting history. The plans for the building, prepared by the governor of Newfoundland, Thomas Cochrane, were at first rejected by the secretary of the colonies, Lord Bathurst. However, Cochrane succeeded in justifying the dimensions of the building by arguing that "in a climate where so large a portion of time must be passed indoors the indulgence of rooms a little larger than might be requisite in a temperate climate may be admissable in a building intended to be permanent and durable." Bathurst accepted the plans, not knowing that Cochrane was subsequently going to add two side wings, alter the hall to make it more imposing, give the stairway a much more elegant appearance and enlarge the portico. These changes to the initial plan were not discovered until the exchequer in London conducted an inquiry into the magnitude of the expenditures for this project. (Public Archives Canada, C 5580)

45 Colonial Building, 78 Military Road, St. John's, Newfoundland

Constructed: 1847-50
Alterations: 1880, 1955-59, 1965
Architect: James Purcell
Material: stone

Since 1955 this building has undergone major alterations considerably changing the composi-tion of its facade, which formerly featured a central frontispiece and a rusticated portico supporting Ionic columns surmounted by a ped-iment.   Despite its late construction, each storey of this building was clearly differen-tiated, in keeping with the Palladian rule. (Canadian Inventory of Historic Building)

46 Customs Building, 150 St. Paul Street, Montreal

Constructed: 1836
Architect: John Ostell
Material: stone

Designed by an architect just returned from studies in England, this building, with its many classical architectural features, undoubtedly received considerable attention, given its location near the market.   Built in 1836 according to plans by John Ostell, the Customs Building clearly shows how the principles of design popularized by the Palladians retained their vitality throughout part of the nineteenth century.   It is also representative of the new interpretation of Palladianism which emerged during 1830-40. This building is more compact than those constructed at the beginning of the century, but the facade is organized along Palladian lines: the ground floor (rather than the basement) is rusticated and features a projecting central section, Tuscan pilasters on the upper storey support a central pediment, the entrance is slightly raised and is accentuated by a portico, and a stone stringcourse demarcates each storey.   Apart from the compactness of the building, there are several decorative motifs that contrast with the sobriety of many earlier buildings: the emblem (no longer present) on the pediment, the cornices and volutes over the windows, the round-headed windows and the Venetian windows. The building was modified in 1855, and again in 1881-82 during which it lost its original dimensions.   The sides were lengthened by 26 feet and given two additional windows on each storey, destroying their symmetry. (Canadian Inventory of Historic Building)

47 Annapolis County Court House, 377 St. George Street, Annapolis Royal, Nova Scotia

Constructed: 1837 by Francis LeCain
Alterations: 1922-23
Architect: Advisory panel, in collaboration with builder Francis LeCain
Material: wood and granite

This building is typical of several small court houses built during this period in Nova Scotia and New Brunswick. Like many such buildings, this one uses a Palladian-inspired architectural formula. The building is designed as a compact block in which each storey constitutes a distinct horizontal division, and on the main floor there are columns supporting a triangular pediment. In 1922-23 the building underwent several alterations (a cupola was added to the roof, the walls of the ground floor were covered with stucco and the chimneys were removed), but these did not change the original design. (Canadian Inventory of Historic Building)

48 Bank of Montreal, St. Jacques Street, Montreal

Constructed: 1818
Demolished: 1870
Material: freestone

During his visit to Montreal in the early 1820s, Edward Allen Talbot commented that this bank, situated on St. Jacques Street near Place d'Armes, was the most handsome building, public or private, in the two Canadas. And indeed, this building constructed of freestone in 1818 was elegant. Outside, it looked like a residential building: nothing indicated it was a bank except for the four emblems on the facade, which symbolized agriculture, industry, the arts and commerce, respectively. In form, the building was in the British classical tradition, but its appearance was made more elegant by the addition of certain Palladian motifs, such as a small Doric portico surmounted by a pediment. The organization and form of the openings were derived from the Palladian rule that the windows on the top storey should be square and smaller than those on the lower storeys. The building housed a bank until 1847 and was demolished in 1870 for a post office. (Public Archives Canada, C 16492)

49 Town Clock, George Street, Halifax

Constructed: 1800–1803
Material: wood

In its plan and vertical composition consisting of circular forms diminishing in size, this building is in the Palladian tradition of circular ornamental buildings. Particularly interesting are the columns supporting the extension of the roof of the largest circular section. Apparently, the Duke of Kent requested this building be designed. William Hughes is generally considered to be its architect, although the name of Captain Straton is also mentioned in this regard. (Heritage Recording Services, Parks Canada)

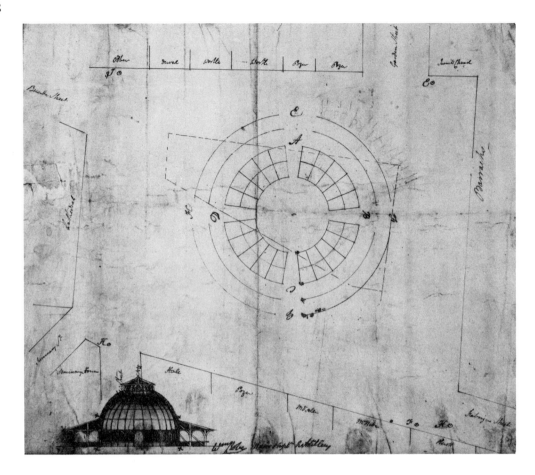

50 **Plan and Elevation of the Upper Town Market Building in Quebec City**

Constructed: 1806
Demolished: ca. 1815
Architect: William Robe
Material: stone and wood

This building, situated in Quebec City's upper town, was constructed according to plans prepared by Major William Robe. A circular stone building, it was crowned with an immense dome and lantern, both of wood. Throughout its brief existence, the building never failed to attract criticism. In about 1806-1808, John Lambert wrote that it was heavy and poorly proportioned. An anonymous contributor to the *Courrier de Québec* (March 1807) wrote that the building was "not in keeping with the rules governing the decoration of public places" (trans.). He added on a humorous note that the initial project had been changed, because "what Mr Robe had in mind was only a flat roof, not far off the ground, with a little dome in the middle — something like a hat with a wide brim; if it had been found unsatisfactory, it would only have taken a kick to send it flying; but as it is, it is likely to collapse on anyone who dares to give it a shake" (trans.). In 1815 Joseph Bouchette indicated that Parliament had ordered the building be demolished for a more appropriate structure. Undeniably, the circular form of this building was dictated by its function, much more than by any aesthetic or stylistic considerations. Nevertheless, its form, as well as its dome and lantern, place it in the tradition of circular ornamental buildings occasionally designed by the Palladians. (Public Archives Canada, C 55344)

51 **Market Building, Queen Square, Charlottetown**

Constructed: 1823
Demolished: ca. 1867
Architect: John Plaw
Material: wood

This market building was the second constructed on Queen Square in Charlottetown. It was built according to a plan prepared in 1819 by English architect John Plaw. Not only was it a circular design, but its ground floor featured twelve round-arched openings. It was covered with a roof extending several feet beyond it, supported by columns. The tiny dome also featured arched openings. The dimensions of this building were much less imposing than those of its counterpart in Quebec City's upper town, constructed some seventeen years earlier (Fig. 50). In November 1842 the building was moved 294 feet northwest to allow for the construction of Province House (Fig. 39). A new market building opened its doors in 1867, and it was probably around this time that the earlier one was demolished. (Public Archives Canada, C 28835)

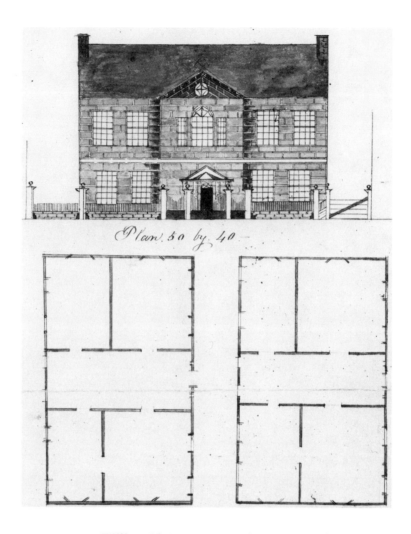

Plan 50 by 40

52 William Dickson House, Niagara, Ontario

Constructed: 1787
Burned down: 1813
Material: brick

William Dickson (1769–1846) emigrated from Scotland to Niagara, where he at first worked for his cousin Robert Hamilton. Subsequently he practised law. During the War of 1812, he was taken prisoner and held captive in the town of Greenbush, New York. On returning to Niagara in January 1816, he discovered that his house, along with the rest of the town, had burned down in 1813. His application for compensation provides a valuable description of his lost home: "For a Brick house, two storeys high, with lofty garrets above and cellar below, partioned with a Brick court yard fence in front agreeably to sketch...." Construction of this house may have begun in 1787. It was completed by 1793, for Dickson wrote then that he had built the first brick house in Upper Canada. It was also the first house in this area to feature on its facade a central frontispiece surmounted by a pediment. The ornamentation concentrated in this projecting section (namely, the circular window in the pediment and the Venetian window) accentuated the central vertical portion of the house. (Public Archives Canada, National Map Collection, C 85688)

Pidgeon House.

ELEVATION & View of MARYVILLE LODGE *from the West*

Scale of Feet

53 Maryville Lodge, Toronto

Constructed: 1794 (demolished)
Material: wood

In 1805 D.W. Smith (1764-1837) wrote the following regarding his house, which he was then trying to sell to C.B. Wyatt, his successor as head surveyor: "I know of no inconvenience my cottage possesses, having built it at a great expence for my own comfort, and without the smallest view of ever selling it; yet you are not to find it a house finished in the style of Architecture which is so good in England; I mean as to finish in point of workmanship and materials...." Despite this rather negative commentary on the style of this house, it features a fairly original device: the pilasters supporting the pediment create the illusion that part of the facade is projected. Also, it has only one storey, unlike most of the houses similarly constructed during this period. (Metropolitan Toronto Library Board)

54 John Strachan House, Front Street West, Toronto

Constructed: 1818
Demolished: 1896
Material: brick

From the time of its completion in 1818, the residence of John Strachan (1778-1867) elicited favourable comment. The house was noted for its imposing dimensions — it had a row of seven windows across the front — and its fashionable stylistic features (central pediment, pilasters and portico). The house reflected the importance of its owner, who at the time was highly influential in religion and education in Upper Canada. Like several large houses built during this period in York, this one was designed to concentrate the main stylistic motifs in its central axis. The pilasters give the impression that there is a frontispiece. Strachan inhabited this house, known as "the Palace," until his death in November 1867; it later became a rooming house and was demolished in 1896. (Metropolitan Toronto Library Board)

55 The Grange, 317 Dundas Street West, Toronto

Constructed: ca. 1817
Alterations: ca. 1840, ca. 1870
Material: brick

The residence of D'Arcy Boulton (1759-1834), solicitor general of Upper Canada, like other large houses in York at the beginning of the nineteenth century, was brick and featured a frontispiece surmounted by a triangular pedi- ment enclosing an oculus. The centre door had a semicircular transom above and long win- dows on either side. Over the years, various changes made to the building accentuated its monumental character. In the 1840s a wing was added to the east side and in about 1885 Dr. Goldwin Smith replaced the wooden porti- co with a stone one and added a library to the west side. (Canadian Inventory of Historic Building)

56 William Campbell House, 160 Queen Street West, Toronto

Constructed: 1822
Material: brick

This residence was constructed in 1822 for Justice William Campbell of the Court of King's Bench. In form and design, it recalls other houses built in York during the same period, such as those of D'Arcy Boulton (ca. 1817) and John Strachan (1818) (Figs 55, 54, respectively). What distinguishes Campbell's house from the other two is the semielliptical transom over the main door. The introduction of this Neoclassical element in a basically Palladian facade marks a new stage in the evolution of domestic architecture. (Canadian Inventory of Historic Building)

57 264 King Street East, Kingston, Ontario

Constructed: 1825-26
Material: stone

This house illustrates well how the Palladian-inspired facade design featuring a central frontispiece, initially used for large homes, was subsequently applied to houses of more modest dimensions. This square stone house, with only three openings on its facade, has a central projection surmounted by a tiny pediment. Also noteworthy are the quoins, which were rarely used in this type of construction and which attest to the persistence of Baroque traditions popularized by James Gibbs. (Canadian Inventory of Historic Building)

58 320 Dibble Street, Prescott, Ontario

Constructed: 1827
Material: stone

This house illustrates one way in which the architectural formula of a frontispiece with pediment was transformed. The spacing of the stone stringcourses on the facade gives the impression that there is a frontispiece. At the same time, the pediment crowning the building perpetuates a Palladian device. Also integrated into the facade are Neoclassical elements: the fanlight in the pediment and its semielliptical counterpart over the main door. (Canadian Inventory of Historic Building)

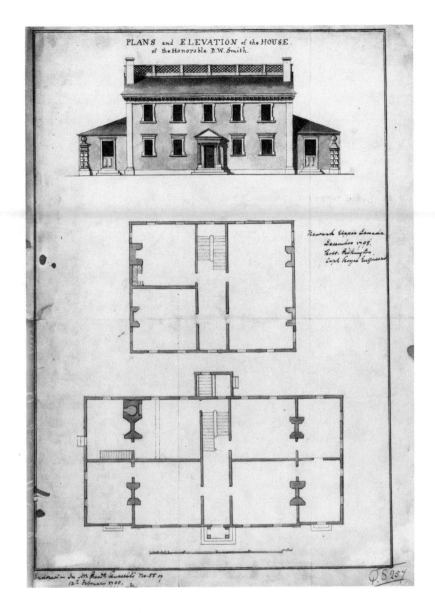

PLANS and ELEVATION of the HOUSE.
of the Honorable D.W.Smith.

59 William Smith House, Niagara-on-the-Lake, Ontario

Constructed: ca. 1798
Burned down: 1813
Architect: Captain Robert Pilkington

This house belonged to William Smith (1764–1837) and the plans and elevations for it were prepared by Captain Robert Pilkington, Royal Engineer. It was the first house in Upper Canada with a central block flanked by two lateral wings. The few decorative motifs that adorn this relatively simple and austere structure give it a certain elegance: the pilasters framing the central portion of the building, the mouldings around the windows, the balustrade running along the roof, and the small pediment and pilasters framing the door. (Public Archives Canada, NMC-6244)

60 Alexander Fraser House, Fraserfield, Ontario

Constructed: ca. 1812
Material: stone

A native of Scotland, Alexander Fraser (ca. 1785–1853) was an officer during the War of 1812. At the end of hostilities, he settled in Fraserfield, in Glengarry County. There he built a home expressing perfectly the Palladian precepts of harmony and symmetry. The central block of the building, with its five openings, is flanked by lower side wings. Tall chimneys punctuate the ends of the roof, and a cupola adorns the centre of the main roof. (Public Archives Canada, PA 51902)

61 Belle Vue, 525 Dalhousie Street, Amherstburg, Ontario

Constructed: 1816-19
Alterations: nineteenth century
Material: brick

Constructed between 1816 and 1819 for the associate commissioner general, Robert Reynolds, this residence is the best example in Upper Canada of lateral wings framing a central block. Originally the two wings were linked to the central building by corridors, a device associated with mansions in England or certain southern American states. Unfortunately, the various alterations have masked the building's original design. (Canadian Inventory of Historic Building)

62 Laurent Quetton de St. George House, 204 King Street East, Toronto

Constructed: 1807-1808
Demolished: 1904
Material: brick

Laurent Quetton de St. George (?-1821) was a French royalist officer who immigrated to Canada in 1798. He first settled in Windham, Markham County, north of York. He went into the fur trade and soon became wealthy. In 1802 he opened a store in York and subsequently established branches in Orillia, Niagara and Amherstburg. In 1807-1808 he had a house built for himself in York, reminis-cent of certain models provided by the architectural treatises (such as the first writings of Asher Benjamin or those of Robert Morris). The massive, rectangular form of the building placed it in the British classical tradition, but certain motifs such as the Venetian window on the second floor, the centre door framed by side windows, and the little portico, gave this building a highly refined appearance. As in several other houses built then, the Palladian influence was also evident in the treatment of the openings. (Metropolitan Toronto Library Board)

63 Homewood, Maitland, Ontario

Constructed: 1800-1801
Material: stone

This house was built for one of the first physicians in Ontario, Dr. Salomon Jones (1756-1822). A native of Connecticut, Dr. Jones studied medicine in Albany, New York, and in 1776, during the American Revolution, he joined the British forces. In 1784 Jones obtained a 500-acre grant in the township of Augusta and built a log house there in 1799. In 1800-1801 he had this stone house built by Louis Brillière, a master mason from the St-Antoine district of Montreal. Like several other buildings in this part of Ontario (see Fig. 29), Dr. Jones's house combines aspects of several architectural traditions. A tripartite window with a flat lintel is situated above the central door, accentuated by a rectangular transom and small side lights. The existing portico is a recent addition, replacing a small portico with six columns surmounted by a pediment. These three components — window, door and original portico — accentuate the central vertical axis of the building as popularized by Palladian architecture. By contrast, the steeply pitched, two-sloped roof and the fieldstone masonry denote the influence of Quebec architecture, which may certainly be explained by the origin of the builder. (Canadian Inventory of Historic Building)

112

64 **Gladys Dudley, Maitland, Ontario. Constructed** ca. 1821 **Material** stone
(Canadian Inventory of Historic Building)

65 **113 Johnson Street, Kingston, Ontario. Constructed** ca. 1825 **Material** stone
(Canadian Inventory of Historic Building)

66 **126 Johnson Street, Niagara-on-the-Lake, Ontario. Constructed** ca. 1830 **Material** wood
(Canadian Inventory of Historic Building)

These houses illustrate the classical ornamentation popularized by Palladianism incorporated into various small vernacular buildings in Ontario. On all these houses, the front door is the only part of the facade that reflects this influence. Each door represents an original adaptation of certain devices widely popularized by the books of models: one door is surmounted by a rectangular transom, another by a semicircular transom, and a third by a small pediment with pilasters on either side.

67 Maplelawn, 529 Richmond Road, Ottawa

Constructed: 1831
Material: stone

This house is modelled on an architectural type introduced by the Loyalists and reflected in homes along the St. Lawrence and Ottawa rivers and in the Atlantic region. Maplelawn is two and a half storeys and made of cut stone, with a hipped roof bordered by chimneys on either side, a facade with five openings, and a central door. This type of house belongs to the great British classical tradition and examples of it are found in England, dating from the era in which Baroque architecture was popular, as well as from the Palladian and Neoclassical periods. Books of models — particularly those produced during the Palladian period — did much to popularize and disseminate this architectural type, not only in England but also in the colonies. As in Maplelawn, the outside ornamentation on these houses was usually limited to the door and was often an adaptation of the classical vocabulary popularized by the books. Here the door is surmounted by a Neoclassical semielliptical transom and flanked by Neoclassical side lights. (Heritage Recording Services, Parks Canada)

68 Robert Millen House, Bay Street, Toronto

Constructed: 1826 (demolished)
Material: wood

This little wooden cottage cannot be associated with any particular architectural current. However, the ornamentation surrounding the door is an exceptional example of the influence of the classical vocabulary. The owner and builder, Robert Millen, a native of Belfast, Ireland, and a carpenter by trade, has made a highly personal statement with classical motifs. As in several other small wooden or stone houses, the classical vocabulary popularized by both Palladianism and Neoclassical architecture is adapted and applied here liberally. (Metropolitan Toronto Library Board)

69 T.A. Coffin House, St. Louis Street, Quebec City

Constructed: 1795-97 (demolished)
Material: stone

This elegant residence, situated on St. Louis Street, was constructed for the Loyalist Thomas Aston Coffin (1754–1810), who at the time was comptroller of accounts for Lower Canada. Of the various buildings on this street as shown in an engraving by James Patterson Cockburn, this one is notable be- cause of a projecting frontispiece and an en- closed portico. The main elements of its ornamentation are located on the central por- tion of the facade. The pediment contains an oculus and the portico, surmounted by a small pediment, features three doors with semicir- cular transoms. An unusual touch is that the two windows adjacent to the door are framed by Ionic pilasters. (Public Archives Canada, C 10655)

70 Spencer Wood, St. Louis Road, Quebec City

Constructed: ca. 1780
Burned down: 1860
Material: wood

This famous residence built on the property of General Henry Watson Powell (1733-1814), overlooking the St. Lawrence River, exhibited some of the most popular elements of the Palladian style. The central block of the house was flanked by side pavilions linked by corridors. A frontispiece featuring an oculus and a small portico accentuated the main entrance. General Powell was the owner until 1796, hence the name, Powell Place. One of the building's owners, a tax collector named Michael Henry Perceval, named it Spencer Wood in honour of a relative, Spencer Perceval, a British prime minister assassinated in 1812. Henry Atkinson purchased the house in 1833 and made various alterations to it. Finally, in 1854, it passed into the hands of the Canadian Government. It burned down in 1860. (Royal Ontario Museum)

71 Caldwell Manor, Etchemin River, Quebec

Constructed: early nineteenth century
        (demolished)
Material: wood (?)

A native of Ireland, Henry Caldwell (1738-1810) came to this country with the English troops. In 1801 he acquired the seignory of Lauzon from the estate of General James Murray; there he had sawmills built to export timber from his properties to England. Probably not long after acquiring the seignory, Caldwell had this imposing house built at the mouth of the Etchemin River, opposite Sillery. The painting by Joseph Légaré shows us a rather exceptional dwelling reminiscent of certain large country houses in England. The building's central block, flanked by lateral wings, features a central frontispiece surmounted by a triangular pediment. On the upper storey, this pediment is supported by pilasters resting on a monumental portico with four Doric columns. Pilasters also frame the central block and the lateral wings. (Musée du Québec)

72 Rolland Manor, 625 des Hurons Road West, St-Mathias, Quebec

Constructed: ca. 1826-30
Material: wood

Built by Jean-Roch Rolland (1785-1862) in his seignory of Ste-Marie de Monnoir, this house is one of the best examples in Quebec of a central block flanked by lateral wings. The use of the two wings, along with two small stone buildings adjacent to the house, shows a genuine concern for harmonious proportions and symmetry, also evident in the relationship of each part of the building to the whole and that of the two stone outbuildings to the house. The plan and composition of this building represent exceptional architectural achievement recalling certain houses in the United States (Mount Airy, 1758-62, Richmond County, Virginia). (Heritage Recording Services, Parks Canada)

73 St. Antoine Hall, 1322–1338 Torrance Street, Montreal

Constructed: 1823
Alterations: 1839
Destroyed: ca. 1968
Material: stone

The central portion of merchant John Torrance's house was constructed in 1823. On March 1, 1823 Torrance concluded an agreement with carpenter Charles Hogg in which the house was to measure 50 by 36 feet and have dormers. The roof was to project to cover the gallery at the rear. The front and rear facades were to have "venetian doors with side and fanlight similar to the same in Mr. Pothier's house and not inferior to it." It was also stated that Dr. Robertson's house on St. James Street and John Torrance's house on St. Paul Street would serve as models in the event of disagreement. On March 8, 1839 John Torrance included a new agreement with master masons William Hutchison and James Morrison for the construction of two stone wings for his house, according to plans by architect John Ostell. An agreement concluded on the same day with carpenter James Telfer reveals that "windows on main floor were to be venetian sashes (three compartiments) two inch fancy molded english sashes." This house was thus constructed in two stages: the central section, built in 1823, was similar in form and ornamentation to other Montreal residences of a certain scale. The addition of the side wings in the late 1830s is a rather late use of a Palladian-inspired composition. However, the ornamentation on these two wings — particularly the arcades — denotes the Neoclassical influence. (Public Archives Canada, C 23085)

74 Jonathan Sewell House, 87 St. Louis Street, Quebec City

Constructed: 1803-1804
Material: stone

This house belonged to Jonathan Sewell (1766-1839), chief justice of Lower Canada for thirty years. Even today this house belongs to the tradition of British classicism, as seen not only in the overall sober and austere appearance, but more particularly in the compact form, the symmetrically placed five openings on each storey, the gently pitched, two-sloped roof, and the raised central entrance. When constructed, this building was noteworthy for its Palladian architectural elements (which disappeared during the nineteenth century): a semicircular transom over the centre door, and side pavilions linked to the house by walls or perhaps corridors. One of these pavilions disappeared, and the other was incorporated into the walls of the Garrison Club. (Canadian Inventory of Historic Building)

75 Monklands, 4245 Décarie Boulevard, Montreal

Constructed: 1803
Alterations: 1844
Material: stone

Built in 1803 by James Monk (1745–1826), chief justice of the Court of King's Bench, this house became the official residence of the governor general in 1844 and the Villa Maria Convent in 1854. Various changes made to the building from 1844 onward tended to modify or even eliminate the Palladian-inspired motifs which may be seen in a watercolour painted in 1813 by George Heriot. At that time the two-storey building had a compact, massive appearance lightened by the raised portico, reached by lateral stairways. The basement was raised, and the openings were spaced in an orderly, symmetrical manner. Quoins decorated the ends of the walls, keeping the Baroque tradition taken up by James Gibbs. (Public Archives Canada, C 10680)

76 540 Salaberry Street East, Mercier, Quebec

Constructed: early nineteenth century
Material: stone

This house is considered to have belonged to the Hudson's Bay Company at the beginning of the nineteenth century. It is then thought to have become the property of Alexis Sauvageau, a captain in the Beauharnois Division in 1812, and subsequently to have been passed on to his son Tancrède, a merchant and distiller. In 1851 the house passed into the hands of Jane Douglass Sweeny, the widow of William Caldwell, one of the founders of the Montreal General Hospital. The form of the building, as well as its roof, is reminiscent of houses in the British classical tradition. Like several houses built at the beginning of the nineteenth century, this one incorporates Palladian elements. Its facade features a small, triangular pediment enclosing a semicircular window. Over the main entrance is a door designed to look like a Venetian window, opening onto a small balcony. The door and the balcony may be of more recent construction than the rest of the building. (Heritage Recording Services, Parks Canada)

77 **Johnson Manor, St-André d'Argenteuil, Quebec. Constructed** early nineteenth century **Destroyed** 1885 **Material** brick (Public Archives Canada, C 19143)

78 **Johnson Manor, St-Mathias, Quebec. Constructed** early nineteenth century **Material** stone (Public Archives Canada, PA 36805)

79 Mount Johnson, Johnstown, New York. Constructed 1763 by Samuel Fuller
Material wood (New York State Parks and Recreation)

After the American Revolution, Sir John Johnson (1742-1830) left the United States to settle at St-André d'Argenteuil, the seignory he had acquired. There he had a brick house built for himself at the turn of the nineteenth century. Its form and dimensions were reminiscent of the British classical tradition. It was a rectangular block with five openings on its facade and a hipped roof with a chimney on either side (Fig. 77). The main door, with its semielliptical transom and side lights, showed the influence of Neoclassical architecture, which was beginning to manifest itself. Several years later, Johnson built another house of the same form at St-Mathias de Rouville, this time of stone (Fig. 78). It too was a rectangular two-storey building with five openings on its facade and a hipped roof adorned with four tall chimneys on the sides. Unlike the house at St-André d'Argenteuil, this one is still standing, although it has undergone various alterations over the years. Both these houses built by Sir John Johnson are thought to be copies of Johnson Hall, the family home located in the Mohawk River valley. However, a second Johnson family property in New York State offers more similarities with the houses in St-Mathias and St-André d'Argenteuil. Mount Johnson (also called Fort Johnson) (1741-43) is a rectangular stone building with five openings on its facade and a hipped roof with dormers and tall chimneys (Fig. 79).

80 **William Lunn House, 4 du Parc Avenue, Montreal**

Constructed: ca. 1820
Alterations: 1879-1912
Demolished: ca. 1920
Material: stone

William Lunn emigrated from England in 1819 to Montreal, where he was placed in charge of the naval stores of the British admiralty. He also played a major role in the educational and political life of Montreal. He helped organize a system of public education for the city's English-speaking population, became a magistrate in 1826, and from 1840 to 1850 served on the city council. We do not know when this building, situated on the northeast corner of Sherbrooke Street and Park Avenue, was constructed or by whom. Lunn may have acquired it when he married Margaret Fisher, William Hutchison's widow, in 1821. Judging from the form and major features of this building, it was constructed around 1820. Like several other houses built in the Montreal area then, it was rectangular, with a hipped roof and five openings on its facade. The double portico on the facade may have been added at the end of the nineteenth century for we know additions were made to the house between 1879 and 1912. (Notman Photographic Archives, McCord Museum)

81 **Couillard de l'Espinay Manor, Montmagny, Quebec**

Constructed: ca. 1814
Material: stone

On March 25, 1814 Antoine-Gaspard Couillard concluded an agreement with a mason named Joseph Petitclaire to construct a stone house in the parish of St. Thomas and it may be the one shown. Subsequently, William Randall Patton acquired the property and had a brick flour mill constructed on it. Like several houses built for prominent people then, this building conforms to the great British classical tradition. It has a rather gently pitched hipped roof flanked by two chimneys. Its facade has five openings and the central door is framed by small rectangular windows, in keeping with the Palladian style. The double portico accentuating the building's monumentality is a later addition. (Heritage Recording Services, Parks Canada)

82 Charles-Michel de Salaberry House, 18 Richelieu Street, Chambly, Quebec

Constructed: 1814-15 by Pierre Papineau (at beginning of construction)
Material: stone

This stone house was built in 1814-15 in the seignory of Chambly by the hero of Châteauguay, Charles-Michel d'Irumberry de Salaberry (1778-1829). Like several other homes built then in the Montreal area, it has British classical features: a rectangular form, five openings on its facade, a hipped roof and two side chimneys. The double portico with its pediment is a later addition. The builder's contract concluded on May 16, 1814 between Salaberry and a master joiner named Pierre Papineau does not mention a double portico, but instead refers to a gallery or flight of steps, as well as two stone pediments to be situated over walls, one in front and the other in the rear. (Heritage Recording Services, Parks Canada)

**83 51 St. Louis Street, Quebec City
Constructed** ca. 1833–34 **Material** stone
(Canadian Inventory of Historic Building)

84 **40 Ste-Angèle Street, Quebec City
Constructed** 1815 by Edward Cannon **Material**
stone (Canadian Inventory of Historic Building)

Several houses built in Quebec City during the
1820s show the Palladian influence. In some
cases, this influence is expressed in the hierarchical organization of openings: those on
the ground floor and the second floor are
rectangular, while those on the top floor are
smaller and square (Fig. 83); the Palladian
architects recommended the windows of the
top floor be smaller than those on the lower
floors, since rooms on this floor are used for
study or sleep and require little light. Another
manifestation of the Palladian influence is the
use of classical decorative motifs (Fig. 84),
generally concentrated around the door.

85 **37 Ste-Ursule Street, Quebec City**

Constructed: ca. 1802 by Richard Goldsworthy
Material: stone

A native of Cornwall in England, Richard Goldsworthy settled in Quebec City following the American Revolution. His house illustrates Palladian motifs integrated into traditional Quebec architecture. The house is one and a half storeys, typical of the Quebec building style. The front door, at the centre of the facade, is surmounted by a semicircular transom and framed by Ionic pilasters supporting a Doric entablature. This Palladian door treatment apparently was very popular in Quebec City at the turn of the nineteenth century. (Heritage Recording Services, Parks Canada)

86 Naval Commissioner's House, Halifax

Constructed: ca. 1785
Demolished: 1909
Material: wood

This imposing house belonged to the naval commissioner in Halifax. Probably because of its wood construction, it resembles certain houses in New England. In the Atlantic region, wood was commonly used in domestic architecture, and it did not prevent the builder from reproducing fairly faithfully some of the stylistic motifs generally associated with stone structures. The corners of this house are ornamented with wooden imitations of stone quoins, and it was one of the first in the Atlantic region with a projecting central frontispiece. Except for Gorsebrook in Halifax (ca. 1811-22, demolished in 1959), Belle Vue in Halifax (demolished) and Norway House in Pictou (ca. 1814, altered in the late nineteenth century), this architectural device apparently was used seldom here. The upper storey of the frontispiece on the commissioner's house features a Venetian window. The rear facade also has a central frontispiece. Also noteworthy are the rectangular form of this building and the hipped roof with its widow's walk, dormers and tall side chimneys, all typical features of buildings of this period. (Nova Scotia Museum)

87 **Mount Uniacke, Lakeland, Nova Scotia**

Constructed: 1813-15
Material: wood

This elegant residence was built for Richard John Uniacke, solicitor general of Nova Scotia from 1797 to 1830. A native of Ireland employed as a clerk at Fort Cumberland, Uniacke was arrested in 1776 on suspicion of sympathizing with the American rebels. Apparently while being taken to Halifax to stand trial, he became entranced by the beauty of the lake and forests at Lakeland and promised himself that he would one day build a home there. His trial did not take place, and subsequently he returned to Ireland to study law. On returning to Halifax, he obtained a 1000-acre land grant, including the site that had enchanted him several years earlier. However, it was not until 1813 that he managed to carry out his project. He named his house Mount Uniacke in memory of the family home in Ireland. Mount Uniacke is particularly noteworthy for its raised basement and its monumental portico, covering both storeys of the building. This portico, with its four columns and wide, projecting pediment enclosing a semicircular window, is unequalled in the colony and is reminiscent of the porticos adorning mansions in the American South. Because of this monumental portico, Mount Uniacke definitely conforms to some of Palladio's models for country houses (for example, plate XXXI of the *Quattro Libri dell'Architettura*). The central door is surmounted by a semicircular transom and flanked by windows. Pilasters adorn the ends of the walls. Several alterations were made to the building over the years: the columns supporting the portico were replaced with square pillars, and the flat roof was replaced with a hipped roof. (Heritage Recording Services, Parks Canada)

88 17 Edgewater Street, Mahone Bay, Nova Scotia

Constructed: 1799
Material: wood

The addition of lateral wings to a rectangular central building was popular in the Atlantic region and several examples of this Palladian feature have survived. This house consists of a central section flanked by two symmetrical wings (probably not original). The central door, surmounted by a small rectangular transom and a pediment with a return, conforms to the Palladian book models. (Canadian Inventory of Historic Building)

89 129 Central Street, Chester, Nova Scotia

Constructed: ca. 1800
Material: wood

This wooden house is ornamented in front and in the rear with a wide triangular pediment enclosing an oculus. These pediments helped to concentrate the entire effect of the design on the central vertical axis of the facade. The two lateral wings which extend the building's central block enhance the symmetry of the design, in keeping with the Palladian precept. The door, with its semielliptical transom and side lights, is Neoclassical. Thus over the years, a variety of influences have left their mark on the original building — a clear indication of the appeal of new architectural trends. This house is fairly representative of wooden buildings that have undergone more changes than stone structures precisely because of the nature of the building material. (Canadian Inventory of Historic Building)

90 **Bloomfield, 2730 Fuller Terrace, Halifax**

Constructed: ca. 1838
Material: wood

A man named Hugh Bell had this house built for himself. A native of Ireland who settled in Nova Scotia at an early age, he was elected to the Halifax town council in 1841 and became mayor in 1844. His wooden house clearly illustrates the way in which certain Palladian motifs were used in the Atlantic region. The facade of the building features a central frontispiece with a semicircular window. Contrary to older buildings, the cornice on the pediment is not closed but open. Small lateral wings added not long after the original construction complement the central section of the building and give it a more harmonious appearance. (Canadian Inventory of Historic Building)

91 Keillor House, 12 Sackville Road, Dorchester, New Brunswick

Constructed: ca. 1813
Material: stone

This house, located in Dorchester, between Moncton and Sackville, was built by John Keillor. A native of Yorkshire, England, Keillor first brought his family to Fort Beauséjour. Later he obtained a concession of land in Dorchester and soon became an influential member of his community. The house he had built is one of the rare stone buildings in the Atlantic region to use this type of design. However, note that the lateral wings are not identical. The treatment of the stone on the facade clearly differentiates one storey from the other. (Canadian Inventory of Historic Building)

92 Acacia Grove, Starr's Point, Nova Scotia

Constructed: ca. 1811-17
Material: brick

A native of Halifax, Charles Ramage Prescott (1772-1859) was a prosperous merchant and a member of the Legislative Assembly for the township of Cornwallis (1825-38). He was noted mainly for his contributions in horticulture, particularly his efforts to promote apple growing in the Annapolis Valley. The house he built at Starr's Point in the Annapolis Valley, moreover, was located on orchard land. It is a brick structure, standing on a stone foundation, with five openings on its facade and a slightly curved hipped roof punctuated by two massive chimneys. The front door has a semielliptical transom and side lights and is sheltered by a small portico. This house is one of the best-preserved examples of this architectural type, derived from the British classical tradition and disseminated through the Palladian treatises. Its interior layout is equally interesting because it follows the plan proposed by the books of models: on the ground floor there is a double central hall surrounded by the reception room, the dining room and the library. (Heritage Recording Services, Parks Canada)

93 **Admiralty House, Halifax**
Constructed 1815–ca. 1819 **Material** stone
(Canadian Inventory of Historic Building)

Elevation toward the West.

From Adm Sec, In Letters, Vol 504, p 625.

Copied by C.Pettigrew at P.R.O. Oct. 1918.

[Proposed house for the Admiral of the Station, at Halifax. Oct. 1813]

94 **Proposed Elevation for Admiralty House, Halifax**
Architect John Plaw **Date** 1813 (Public Archives Canada, C 94090)

About 1812 the imperial government authorized spending £3,000 to construct a house for the commander-in-chief of the North American naval base at Halifax and two years later increased the amount. The five-acre lot, adjacent to the shipyards, was purchased in 1814. Constructed between 1815 and about 1819, Admiralty House, despite the various alterations it has since undergone, remains an interesting example of British classical architecture. It is a two-and-a-half-storey stone building with a medium-sloped hipped roof, three dormers, a pediment in the front and rear, and five rectangular openings on the facade. The closed portico, surmounted by a pediment with dentils, is an addition probably dating from the early twentieth century. The roof extends slightly beyond the building line, and the frieze is adorned with dentils. Inside, the rooms are arranged around a central hall, with two deep rooms on either side. English architect John Plaw (1745?-1820) proposed plans and elevations for this building in 1813 (Fig. 94). His Neoclassical-inspired elevations were lavish: the front facade was adorned with oval windows and pilasters, and the rear facade featured Venetian windows and arcades. No doubt the government considered this proposal too ambitious and costly and preferred a more traditional design.

95 Loyalist House, 120 Union Street, Saint John, New Brunswick

Constructed: ca. 1817
Material: wood

This elegant wooden house was built by David Daniel Merritt, the son of an American Loyalist from Rye, New York. Typical of houses in the British classical tradition built at the turn of the nineteenth century, it is a rectangular, two-storey building with five openings on its facade, and a hipped roof adorned with four tall chimneys. The basement is raised much higher than usual, and two lateral stairways provide access to the front door. Here again the use of clapboard siding links this house with certain houses in New England. This is one of the few buildings to have survived the Saint John fire of 1877. It was restored during the 1950s. (Canadian Inventory of Historic Building)

96 Crane House, 7 East Main Street, Sackville, New Brunswick

Constructed: ca. 1830
Material: stone

This house represents a new stage in the treatment of the form derived from the British classical tradition. It is much more refined than older houses of the same type. Its roof is less steeply pitched than that of Admiralty House (Fig. 93) and the treatment of the stone is also different. Furthermore, the Neoclassical influence is visible, in the building's more imposing dimensions, the presence of a central window on the upper storey, and the treatment of the front door. (Canadian Inventory of Historic Building)

97 **18 Fort Lawrence Road, Fort Lawrence, Nova Scotia**
Constructed ca. 1775-80 **Material** brick (Canadian Inventory of Historic Building)

98 **Kingston, Nova Scotia**
Constructed ca. 1790 **Material** wood (Canadian Inventory of Historic Building)

99 Dyke Road, Upper Falmouth, Nova Scotia
Constructed ca. 1793 **Material** wood (Canadian Inventory of Historic Building)

100 The Ledge, New Brunswick
Constructed ca. 1800 **Material** wood (Canadian Inventory of Historic Building)

101 **78 King Street, St. Andrews, New Brunswick**
Constructed ca. 1825 **Material** wood (Canadian Inventory of Historic Building)

Several vernacular-type houses in the Atlantic provinces, generally wood, incorporated the classical repertoire popularized by Palladianism. The central door was usually the only part of the facade to show this influence. Among the most popular features (and probably the oldest) was the rectangular transom; others were the semicircular transom (with or without entablature), side lights, and the little pediment over the door or transom. In Nova Scotia particularly, the door was often sheltered by a small, closed, projecting portico.

BIBLIOGRAPHY

Acadian Magazine (Halifax)
Article, no title, Vol. 1, No. 3, Sept. 1826, p. 81.

Ackerman, James S.
Palladio. Penguin, Harmondsworth, 1966.

Adams, F. Dawson
A History of Christ Church Cathedral, Montreal. Burton's, Montreal, 1941.

Aide-Mémoire to the Military Sciences Framed from Contributions of Officers of Different Services, and Edited by a Committee of the Corps of Royal Engineers
2nd ed., John Weale, London, 1853, 3 vols.

Algie, Susan
"Reports on Selected Buildings in Ontario." Manuscript on file, National Historic Parks and Sites Branch, Parks Canada, Ottawa, 1979.

Angus, Margaret
The Old Stones of Kingston. Its Buildings Before 1867. University of Toronto Press, Toronto, 1966.

Architects' Emergency Committee
Great Georgian Houses of America. Reprint 1937 ed., Dover, New York, 1970, 2 vols.

Architecture de Philibert de l'Orme
Reprint 1648 ed., Gregg Press, Ridgewood, New Jersey, 1964.

Arthur, Eric R.
"The Early Architecture of the Province of Ontario." The Journal Royal Architectural Institute of Canada, Vol. 5, No. 1 (Jan. 1928), p. 25, Ottawa.
—. Toronto. No Mean City. University of Toronto Press, Toronto, 1964.

Atkinson, Christopher William
A Historical and Statistical Account of New-Brunswick, B.N.A. with Advice to Emigrants. Anderson & Bryce, Edinburgh ,1844.

Ball, Jean M.
A Gift of Heritage. Valhalla Press, St. John's, Newfoundland, 1975.

Barrington, Kaye
The Development of the Architectural Profession in Britain. A Sociological Study. George Allen & Unwin, London, 1960.

Bastien, G., D.D. Dubé and C. Southam
"Inventaire des marchés de construction des archives civiles de Québec, 1800-1870." History and Archaeology/Histoire et archéologie, 1a-c (1975). Ottawa.

Bédard, Hélène
Maisons et églises du Québec. Ministère des Affaires culturelles, Quebec, 1972.

Benjamin, Asher
The Country Builder's Assistant: Containing a Collection of New Designs of Carpentry and Architecture. Thomas Dickman, Greenfield, 1797.
—. The Rudiments of Architecture Being a Treatise on Practical Geometry on Grecian and Roman Mouldings. Munroe and Francis, Boston, 1814.

Betcherman, Lita-Rose
"William Von Moll Berczy," MA thesis, Carleton University, Ottawa, 1962.

Bigsby, John J.
The Shoe and Canoe. Or Pictures of Travel in the Canadas. Reprint 1850 ed., Palladin, New York, 1969.

Bill, R., A. Earle and J. Lewis
Reports on Selected Buildings in St. John's, Newfoundland. Manuscript Report No. 256, Parks Canada, Ottawa, 1974.

Bird, Will R.
"Some Historic Houses of Nova Scotia." Canadian Geographical Journal, Vol. 57, No. 2 (Aug. 1952), pp. 62-65. Ottawa.

Blake, Verschoyle Benson and Ralph Greenhill
Rural Ontario. University of Toronto Press, Toronto, 1969.

Bonnycastle, Richard Henry
Canada and the Canadians in 1846. Henry Colburn, London, 1846, 2 vols.

Bosworth, Newton
Hochelaga Depicta, or the Early History and
Present State of the City and Island of
Montreal. William Greig, Montreal, 1839.

Bouchette, Joseph
Description topographique de la province du
Bas-Canada, avec des remarques sur le Haut-
Canada et sur les relations des deux provinces
avec les États-Unis de l'Amérique. W. Faden,
London, 1815.

Brigstocke, Rev. Canon
History of Trinity Church Saint John, New-
Brunswick. N.p., Saint John, New Brunswick,
1892.

Brosseau, Mathilde
"Monklands (Villa Maria Convent)," Agenda
Paper, May 1974-H, Historic Sites and Monu-
ments Board of Canada, Ottawa, 1974.

Buell, Augustus C.
Sir William Johnson. Appleton, New York,
1903.

Burns, Florence M.
William Berczy. Fitzhenry and Whiteside, Don
Mills, 1977.

Butcher, Wilfrid F.
"Two Centuries of Presbyterianism in old Quebec." The Presbyterian Record, Vol. 84 (May
1959), p. 12, Toronto.

Cameron, Christina and Jean Trudel
Québec au temps de James Patterson Cockburn. Garneau, Quebec, 1976.

Campbell, Colen
Vitruvius Britannicus or the British Architect
Containing the Plans, Elevations and Sections
of the Regular Buildings both Public and Private in Great Britain..., Jos. Smith, London
[1715]-25, 3 vols.

Campbell, Patrick
Travels in the Interior Inhabited Parts of
North America. In the years 1791 and 1792.
J. Guthrie, Edinburgh, 1793.

Canada. Public Archives
National Map Collection. D340-Québec-1806,
John Bentley report.

H12/340-Québec-1806, plan for a Quebec
market.
MG11, C.O.217, Nova Scotia "A," Vol. 133,
pp..116-19, Sir John Wentworth to the Duke of
Portland, 27 July 1801.
RG1, E12, Reports and Registers, Vol. 2, Pro-
ceedings of the Gaol Commissioners, 1807-
1810.
RG1, E15A, Board of Audit Commissioner,
Vol. 277-79, Commissioners for the erection of
a Metropolitan Church, Quebec, 1760-1804.
RG1, E15A, Board of Audit, Lower Canada,
Vol. 280, Erection of the Montreal Court
House, 1799-1802.
RG1, E15A, Board of Audit, Lower Canada,
Vol. 282-86, Erection of the Quebec Court
House, 1799-1804.
RG1, E15A, Board of Audit, Lower Canada,
Vol. 288-89, Quebec City Gaol, 1808-1817.
RG1, E15A, Board of Audit, Lower Canada,
Vol. 290, Montreal Common Gaol, 1808-1812.

**Catalogue of English and French Books in the
Quebec Library**
N.p., n.p., 1785.

Chabot, Line
Comptes rendus de certains bâtiments dans la
ville de Québec (P.Q.) et dans les municipalités avoisinantes. Travail inédit No. 298,
Parks Canada, Ottawa, 1978.

Clerk, Nathalie
"La maison Prescott à Starr's Point." Manu-
script on file, National Historic Parks and
Sites Branch, Parks Canada, Ottawa, 1980.

Coke, E.T.
A Subaltern's Furlough: Descriptive of Scenes
in Various Parts of the United States, Upper
and Lower Canada, New-Brunswick, and Nova
Scotia, During the Summer and Autumn of
1832. Saunders and Otley, London, 1833.

Colvin, Howard and John Harris, eds.
The Country Seat; Studies in the History of
the British Country House. Penguin, London,
1970.

Courrier de Québec (Le) (Quebec)
Article, no title, 11 March 1807, pp. 2-3.

Cullen, Mary K.
A History of the Structure and Use of Pro-

vince House, Prince Edward Island 1837-1977. Manuscript Report Series No. 211, Parks Canada, Ottawa, 1977.

—. "Charlottetown Market Houses 1813-1958." The Island, No. 6 (spring/summer 1979), pp. 27-32. Charlottetown.

De Jongh Isler, Ariane
"L'ancienne douane de Montréal." Vie des Arts, Vol. 20, No. 79 (summer 1975), p. 39-41. Montréal.

Dendy, William
Lost Toronto.   Oxford University Press, Toronto, 1978.

Doughty, Arthur G.
Report of the Work of the Public Archives for the Years 1914 and 1915.   J. de L. Taché, Ottawa, 1916.

Dounman, C.P.C., ed.
A Concise, Chronological and Factual History of St. Stephen's Anglican Church.   Chambly, Qué. Perry Printing, Montréal, 1970.

Drolet-Dubé, Doris and Marthe Lacombe
"Inventaire des marchés de construction des archives nationales à Québec XVIIe et XVIIIe siècles." History and Archaeology/Histoire et archéologie, 17 (1977), Ottawa.

Eberlein, Harold Donaldson
The Architecture of Colonial America. Reprint 1915 ed., Johnson Reprint, New York, 1968.

Eberlein, Harold Donaldson and Cortland Van Dyke Hubbard
American Georgian Architecture.   Pleiades, London, 1952.

Elliott, Shirley B.
"A History of Province House and Government House." Journal of Education, Vol. 14, No. 1 (Oct. 1964), pp. 42-51. Halifax.

Ferguson, Charles Bruce
"Isaac Hildrith (ca. 1741-1807) Architect of Government House, Halifax." Dalhousie Review, Vol. 51, No. 4 (winter 1970/1971), pp. 510-16, Halifax.

Field, H. and M. Bunney
English Domestic Architecture of the XVII and XVIII Centuries. Bell & Sons, London, 1928.

Galarneau, P.J. Hallé and D. Lapierre
Comptes rendus de certains bâtiments dans la ville de Montréal (P.Q.) et dans les municipalités avoisinantes. Travail inédit No. 300, Parks Canada, Ottawa, 1978.

Gallet, Michel
Demeures parisiennes à l'époque de Louis XVI. Le Temps, Paris, 1964.

Gauthier, Raymonde
Les manoirs du Québec. Fides, Quebec, 1976.

Gazette de Québec (La) (Quebec)
"Catalogue de livres à vendre à l'imprimerie à Québec," 6 Sept. 1787, p. 4 .

Georgian Period, The.   A collection of Papers Dealing with 'colonial' or XVIII Century Architecture in the United States
American Architect & Building News, Boston, 1899.

Gibbs, James
A Book of Architecture Containing Designs of Buildings and Ornaments.   Reprint 1st ed. (1728), Benjamin Blom, New York, 1968.
—.   Rules for Drawing the Several Parts of Architecture. W. Bowyer, London, 1732.

Giroux, André et al.
"Inventaire des marchés de construction des Archives nationales du Québec à Montréal, 1800-1830." Manuscript on file, National Historic Parks and Sites Branch, Parks Canada, Ottawa, 1978. (Now published in History and Archaeology/Histoire et archéologie, 49, 2 vols.)

Gobeil-Trudeau, Madeleine and Luc Noppen
"La chapelle de la congrégation Notre-Dame de Québec." Annales d'Histoire de l'Art Canadien, Vol. 3, Nos. 1-2 (fall 1976), pp. 73-83. Montréal.

Gowans, Allan
Building Canada.   Oxford University Press, Toronto, 1966.
—.   Church Architecture in New-France. University of Toronto Press, Toronto, 1955.

—. Images of American Living. Four Centuries of Architecture and Furniture as Cultural Expression. J.B. Lippincott, Philadelphia, 1964.

—. Looking at Architecture in Canada. Oxford University Press, Toronto, 1958.

—. "New-England Architecture in Nova Scotia." Art Quarterly, Vol. 25, No. 1 (spring 1962), pp. 7-33. New York.

—. "Thomas Baillairgé and the Quebecois Tradition of Church Architecture." The Art Bulletin, Vol. 34, No. 2 (June 1952), pp. 117-37. Providence, Rhode Island.

Gray, Hugh
Letters from Canada Written During a Residence there in the Years 1806, 1807 and 1808. Longman, Hurst, Rees and Orme, London, 1809.

Greenhill, R., K. MacPherson and D. Richardson
Ontario Towns, Oberon Press, Toronto, 1974.

Guggisberg, F.G.
"The shop." The Story of the Royal Military Academy. Cassell, London, 1902.

Gunn, Rev. Archibald
Sixty-second Anniversary of Greenock Church, St. Andrews, N.B. N.p., Halifax, 1886.

Hale, Anne
"Early Court Houses of Nova Scotia." Manuscript on file, National Historic Parks and Sites Branch, Parks Canada, Ottawa, 1979.

—. The Early Court Houses of New Brunswick. Manuscript Report Series No. 290, Parks Canada, Ottawa, 1977.

Hale, Anne and Nathalie Clerk
"Admiralty House, CFB Halifax, Halifax, Nova Scotia." Agenda Paper 1978-09, Historic Sites and Monuments Board of Canada, Ottawa, 1978.

Halfpenny, William
The Art of Sound Building. Reprint 1725 ed., Benjamin Blom, New York, 1968.

—. Magnum in Parvo; or the Marrow of Architecture. Reprint 1728 ed., Benjamin Blom, New York, 1968.

—. Practical Architecture, or a Sure Guide to the True Working According to the Rules of that Science. T. Bowles, London, 1736.

—. A New and Complete System of Architecture Delineated in a Variety of Plans and Elevations of Designs for Convenient and Decorated Houses. John Brindley, London, 1749.

Haliburton, Thomas Chandler
A General Description of Nova Scotia. Clement H. Belcher, Halifax, 1825.

—. An Historical and Statistical Account of Nova Scotia. Joseph Howe, Halifax, 1829, 2 vols.

Hall, Francis
Travels in Canada and the United States in 1816 and 1817. Longman, Hurst, Rees, Orme and Brown, London, 1818.

Harris, John
Georgian Country Houses. Country Life, Feltham, 1968.

Harris, R.V.
The Church of St. Paul in Halifax, N.S. Ryerson, Toronto, 1949.

Harvey, Daniel Cobb, ed.
Journeys to the Island of St. John or Prince Edward Island 1775-1832. MacMillan, Toronto, 1955.

Hautecoeur, Louis
Histoire de l'architecture classique en France. Rev. and enl. ed., Picard, Paris, 7 vols., Vol. 4.

—. Rome et la Renaissance de l'antiquité à la fin du XVIIIᵉ siècle. Fontemoing, Paris, 1912.

Heriot, George
Travels through the Canadas, Containing a Description of the Picturesque Scenery on Some of the Rivers and Lakes. Richard Phillips, London, 1807.

Heritage Trust of Nova Scotia
Founded Upon a Rock; Historic Buildings of Halifax and Vicinity Standing in 1967. Heritage Trust of Nova Scotia, Halifax, 1967.

—. Seasoned Timbers. Heritage Trust of Nova Scotia, Halifax, 1972, 2 vols.

—. St. Mary's Church, Auburn, N.S. 1790. Heritage Trust of Nova Scotia, Halifax, 1967.

Hitchcock, H.R.
Boston Architecture 1637-1954. Reinhold, New York, 1954.

Hodgins, J. George
The School House; its Architecture, External and Internal Arrangements. Lovell and Gibson, Toronto, 1857.

Hogg, Oliver Frederick Gillilan
The Royal Arsenal: its Background, Origin and Subsequent History. Oxford University Press, London, 1963, 2 vols.

"Homewood, Maitland, Ontario"
Manuscript on file, National Historic Parks and Sites Branch, Parks Canada, Ottawa, n.d.

Hounsome, Eric
Toronto, the Town and Buildings in 1810. Coles, Toronto, 1975.

Howison, John
Sketches of Upper Canada, Domestic, Local, and Characteristic; to Which are Added Practical Details for the Information of Emigrants of Every Class. Oliver and Boyd, Edinburgh, 1821.

Hudson, Timothy Peter
"The Origins of Palladianism in English Eighteenth-Century Architecture," Ph.D. dissertation, Cambridge University, 1974.

Innis, Mary Quayle
Mrs. Simcoe's Diary, MacMillan, Toronto, 1965.

Isler, Ariane
"Le vieux marché et l'ancienne douane dans le vieux Montréal." Term paper, Department of History, University of Montreal, Jan. 1972.

Jack, David Russell
History of St. Andrews Church, St. John, N.B. Barnes, Saint John, New Brunswick, 1913.

Johnson, Dana and Leslie Maitland
"Osgoode Hall," Agenda Paper 1979-50, Historic Sites and Monuments Board, Parks Canada, Ottawa, 1979.

Johnson, Dana and C.J. Taylor
Reports on Selected Buildings in Kingston, Ontario. Manuscript Report No. 261, Parks Canada, Ottawa, 1976-77. 2 vols.

Karel, D., L. Noppen and C. Thibault
François Baillairgé et son oeuvre (1759-1830). Musée du Québec, Quebec, 1975.

"Keillor House Museum, Dorchester, N.B."
Brochure, N.p., n.d.

Kimball, Sidney Fiske
Domestic Architecture of the American Colonies and of the Early Republic. Reprint 1st ed. 1922, Dover, New York, 1966.

Kyte, E.C.
Old Toronto. A Selection of Excerpts from Landmarks of Toronto by John Ross Robertson. MacMillan, Toronto, 1954.

Lambert, John
Travels Through Lower Canada and the United States of North America in the Years 1806, 1807 and 1808. Richard Phillips, London, 1810, 3 vols.

Langley, Batty
A Sure Guide to Builders or the Principles and Practice of Architecture Geometrically Demonstrated and Made Easy for the Use of Workmen in General. J. Wilcock, London, 1729.
---. The Builder's Compleat Chest-Book or Library of Arts and Science. H. Woodfall, London, 1738.
---. The City and Country Builders and Workmans Treasury of Designs or the Art of Drawing and Working the Ornamental Parts of Architecture. Reprint 1st ed. 1745, Gregg International, Farnborough, 1969.

Langley, Batty and Thomas Langley
The Builder's Jewel or, the Youth's Instructor and Workman's Remembrancer. R. Ware, London, 1757.

La Rochefoucauld-Liancourt, François Alexandre Frédéric, duke
Voyage dans les États-Unis d'Amérique, fait en 1795, 1796 et 1797. DuPont, Paris 1799, 8 vols., Vol. 2.

Lee, G. Herbert
An Historical Sketch of the First Fifty Years

of the Church of England in the Province of New-Brunswick 1783-1833. Sun Publications, Saint John, New Brunswick, 1833.

Legge, Arthur E.E.
The Anglican Church in Three Rivers, Quebec. 1768-1956. N.p., n.p., 1956.

Lemoine, Sir James MacPherson
Quebec, Past and Present. A History of Quebec. 1608-1876. A. Côté, Quebec, 1876.

Lessard, Michel and Huguette Marquis
Encyclopédie de la maison québécoise. Éditions de l'Homme, Montreal, 1971.

Little, Bryan
The Life and Work of James Gibbs. 1682-1754. Batsford, London, 1955.

"Loyalist House"
Brochure, n.p., n.d.

Lower Canada. House of Assembly
Journal of the House of Assembly of Lower Canada. From the 28th March to the 3rd June 1799. John Neilson, Quebec, 1799.

MacDermot, H.E.
Christ Church Cathedral. A Century in Retrospect. Gazette Printing, Montreal, 1959.

MacGregor, John
Historical and Descriptive Sketches of the Maritime Colonies of British America. Reprint 1st ed. 1828, S.R. Publishers, Wakefield, Great Britain, 1968.

MacKenzie, Hazel M.
"Classical Architecture in Canada. Province House. Halifax. 1811-1819," Term paper, Carleton University, Ottawa, 1978.

MacKinnon, Ian F.
Settlements and Churches in Nova Scotia 1749-1776. Walker Press, Montreal, 1930 .

MacRae, Marion
The Ancestral Roof. Domestic Architecture of Upper Canada. Clarke, Irwin, Toronto, 1963.

Maitland, Leslie
"The Neoclassical Style in Canadian Architecture." Manuscript on file, National Historic Parks and Sites Branch, Parks Canada, Ottawa, 1980. (Forthcoming publication, "Neoclassical Architecture in Canada," Studies in Archaeology, Architecture and History, Parks Canada, Ottawa, 1984.)

Marsan, Jean-Claude
Montréal en évolution, Montreal, Fides, 1974.

Maurault, Msgr Olivier
Marges d'histoire. Librairie d'Action canadienne-française Montreal , 1929-1930, 3 vols., Vol. 1.
———. "Un professeur d'architecture en 1828." L'Art au Canada (1929), pp. 93-113. Montreal.

Mélanges d'histoire du Canada français offerts au professeur Marcel Trudel
Éditions de l'Université d'Ottawa, Ottawa, 1978.

Morisset, Gérard
L'Architecture en Nouvelle-France. Charrier et Dugal, Quebec, 1949.

———. "Une figure inconnue Jérôme Demers." La Patrie (22 March 1953), pp. 36-37. Montreal.

Morris, Robert
An Essay in Defence of Ancient Architecture; or a Parallel of the Ancient Buildings. D. Browne, London, 1728.
———. Architecture Improved in a Collection of Modern, Elegant and Useful Designs in the Taste of Inigo Jones, Mr. Kent & Co. Robert Sayer, London, 1755.
———. Lectures on Architecture Consisting of Rules Founded on Harmonick and Arithmetical Proportions in Buildings. J. Brindley, London, 1734.
———. Rural Architecture Consisting of Regular Designs of Plans and Elevations for Buildings in the Country...., Reprint 1st ed. 1750, Gregg International, Farnborough, 1971.
———. Select Architecture: Being Regular Designs of Plans and Elevations Well Suited to Both Town and Country. Reprint 1st ed. 1757, intro. Adolf K. Placzek, DaCapo Press, New York, 1973.
———. The Architectural Remembrancer Being a Collection of New and Useful Designs of Ornamental Buildings and Decorations for Parks,

Gardens, Woods, & C. Gregg International, Farnborough, 1971.

Mowat, Grace Helen
The Diverting History of a Loyalist Town. A Portrait of St. Andrew's, New-Brunswick, Fredericton, Brunswick Press, 1953.

Musée du Québec
L'art du Québec au lendemain de la conquête (1760-1790). Ministère des Affaires culturelles, Quebec, 1977.

Myers, J.C.
Sketches on a Tour Through the Northern and Eastern States, The Canadas & Nova Scotia. J.H. Wartmann and Brothers, Harrisonburg, Virginia, 1849.

Newton, Michael
Maplelawn 1831-1979. National Capital Commission, Ottawa, 1979.

Nichols, Frederick Doveton
Palladio's Influence on American Architecture: Palladio in America. Electa, Milan, 1976.

Nilsson, Sten
European Architecture in India 1750-1850. Faber & Faber, London, 1968.

Noppen, Luc
Dossier d'inventaire architectural de la prison de Trois-Rivières. Ministère des Affaires culturelles, Quebec, 1977.

—. François Baillairgé et son oeuvre, 1759-1830. Musée du Québec, Quebec, 1975.
—. "Le renouveau architectural proposé par Thomas Baillairgé au Québec de 1820 à 1850," Ph.D. dissertation, Toulouse-Le Mirail University, France, 1976.
—. "Le rôle de l'abbé Jérôme Demers dans l'élaboration d'une architecture néo-classique au Québec." Annales d'histoire de l'art canadien, Vol. 2, No. 1 (summer 1975), pp. 19-33. Montreal.
—. Les églises du Québec (1600-1850). Fides, Quebec City, 1977.
—. "L'utilisation des maquettes et modèles de l'architecture ancienne du Québec." Annales d'histoire de l'art canadien, Vol. 1, No. 1 (1974), pp. 4-10. Montreal.

Noppen, Luc and John Porter
Les églises de Charlesbourg et l'architecture religieuse au Québec. Ministère des Affaires culturelles, Quebec, 1972.

Nova Scotia. Provincial Archives
Dockyard -- Commissioner's House file.
Government House file.
Province House file.
Town Clock file.

Nova Scotia Royal Gazette (Halifax)
Article, no title, 3 July 1811, p. 2.

O'Dea, F.A.
"Government House." Canadian Collector, Vol. 10, No. 2 (March/April 1975).

"Old Government House. Woodstock House"
Manuscript on file, National Historic Parks and Sites Branch, Parks Canada, Ottawa, n.d.

O'Leary, Thomas
Canadian Letters. Description of a Tour Thro' the Provinces of Lower and Upper Canada, in the Course of the Years 1792 and '93. C.A. Marchand, Montreal, 1912.

Orme, Philibert de l'
Premier tome de l'architecture. Frédéric Morel, Paris, 1567.

Oxford English Dictionary, The
Clarendon Press, Oxford, 1961, 13 vols.

Palladio, Andrea
The Four Books of Architecture. Intro. Adolf K. Placzek, Dover, New York, 1965.

Palmer, John
Journal of Travels in the United States of North America and in Lower Canada Performed in the Year 1817. Sherwood, Neely and Jones, London, 1818.

Peabody, R.S.
"Georgian Houses in New-England." American Architect and Building News, Vol. 2 (Oct. 1877), pp. 338-39, Vol. 3 (Feb. 1878), pp. 54-55. Boston.

Pierson, William H., Jr.
American Buildings and Their Architects. The

Colonial and Neoclassical Styles. Doubleday, New York, 1970.

Plumb, J.H.
England in the Eighteenth Century. Penguin, Aylesbury, 1966.

Porter, John R.
Joseph Légaré 1795-1855. L'oeuvre. National Gallery of Canada, Ottawa, 1978.

Porter, John R. and Léopold Désy
"L'ancienne chapelle des récollets de Trois-Rivières." Bulletin No. 18 (1971), National Gallery of Canada, Ottawa.

Porter, Withworth
History of the Corps of Royal Engineers. Longman, Green, London, 1889, 2 vols.

Provost, H., comp.
"Recensement de la ville de Québec en 1818 par le curé Joseph Signay," Cahiers d'histoire, No. 29 (1976), Quebec.

Québec. Affaires culturelles
Inventaire des biens culturels, Gérard Morisset Papers:

   File of former court house, Quebec.
   Saint-Antoine Church file, Longueuil.
   St.-Andrews Church file, Québec.
   Anglican cathedral file, Québec.
   Court house file, Montreal.
   Lefebvre, House file, Mercier.
   Sauvageau/Sweeny House file.
   François Baillairgé Diary, 1784-1800.

Québec.   Archives nationales du Québec à Québec
Greffe du notaire R. Lelièvre, inventory, 30 May 1808.

Quebec City.   Archives du séminaire de Québec
M-131, tablette 4, Précis d'architecture de Jérôme Demers, 1828.
Polygraphie 19, No. 59, will of Thomas Baillairgé, 5 April 1848.

Quebec City.   Bibliothèque du séminaire de Québec
Inventory made by Dudevant, 1782. Sem. 4, No. 128, report on books left by Abbé

Mathurin Jacrau 30 Aug. 1764, given 15 Nov. 1770.

Ralph [pseud.]
A Critical Review of the Publick Buildings Statues and Ornaments in and About London and Westminster. C. Ackers, London, 1734.

Ramsey, Stanley, C. and J.D.M. Harvey
Small Georgian Houses and their Details. Architectural Press, London, 1972.

Reed, T.A.
"Toronto's early architects." Journal of the Royal Architectural Institute of Canada, Vol. 27, No. 2 (Feb. 1950), pp. 46-48. Ottawa.

Richardson, A.E. and C. Lovett Gill
London Houses From 1660-1820. Batsford, London, 1911.

Richardson, A.J.H.
"Guide to the Architecturally and Historically Most Significant Buildings of the Old City of Québec with a Biographical Dictionary of Architects and Builders and Illustrations." Bulletin of the Association for Preservation Technology. Vol. 2, Nos. 3-4 (1970). Ottawa.

Riendeau, Roger E.
"Campbell House." Manuscript on file, National Historic Parks and Sites Branch, Parks Canada, Ottawa, 1974.

———.   "The Grange." Manuscript on file, National Historic Parks and Sites Branch, Parks Canada, Ottawa, n.d.

Robert, Jacques
Les prisons de Trois-Rivières et de Sherbrooke.   Ministère des Affaires culturelles, Quebec, 1979.

Robertson, Douglas, S., ed.
An Englishman in America, 1785. Being the Diary of Joseph Hadfield. Hunter-Rose, Toronto, 1933.

Roos, Frank J.
Writings on Early American Architecture. An Annotated List of Books and Articles on Architecture Constructed Before 1860 in the Eastern Half of the United States. Ohio State University Press, Columbus, 1943.

Roy, Pierre-Georges
Les vieilles églises de la province de Québec, 1647-1800. L.A. Proulx, Quebec, 1925.
—. Vieux manoirs, vieilles maisons. L.A. Proulx, Quebec, 1927.

St. George Church 1800-1975. Halifax, N.S.
N.p., n.p., n.d.

Sells, A. Lytton
The Paradise of Travellers. The Italian Influence on Englishmen in the Seventeenth Century. Indiana University, Bloomington, 1964.

Silliman, Dr. Benjamin
A Tour to Quebec in the Autumn of 1819. Richard Phillips, London, 1822.

Smyth, David William
A Short Topographical Description of His Majesty's Province of Upper Canada in North America. Reprint 1st ed. 1799, S.R. Publishers, Wakefield, Great Britain, 1969.

Stokes, Peter John
Old Niagara-on-the-Lake. University of Toronto Press, Toronto, 1941.

Stone, William L.
Letters of Brunswick and Hessian Officers During the American Revolution. Joel Munsell's Sons, Albany, New York, 1891.

Summerson, John
Architecture in Britain 1530 to 1830. 5th ed., Penguin, Harmondsworth, England, 1969.
—. Georgian London. Pleiades, London, 1945.
—. The Classical Language of Architecture. British Broadcasting Corporation, London, 1963.

Talbot, Edward Allen
Cinq années de séjour au Canada...Suivies d'un extrait du voyage de M.J.M. Duncan en 1818 et 1819. Boulland, Paris, 1825, 3 vols.
—. Five Year's Residence in the Canadas Including a Tour Through Part of the United States of America in the Year 1823, Longman, Hurst, Rees, Orme, Brown and Green, London, 1824, 2 vols.
—. Voyage au Canada. Librairie Centrale, Paris, 1833, 3 vols., Vol. 1.

Taylor, C.J.
The Early Court Houses of Prince Edward Island. Manuscript Report Series No. 289, Parks Canada, Ottawa, 1977.

Traquair, Ramsay
The Old Architecture of Quebec. MacMillan, Toronto, 1947.

Trudel, Jean
William Berczy. La famille Woolsey. National Gallery of Canada, Ottawa, 1976.

Turnor, Reginald
The Smaller English House, 1500-1939. Batsford, London, 1952.

University of New Brunswick, Fredericton.
Harriet Irving Library Archives. Arts Building, Documents, Nos. 382-85.

Vardy, John
Some Designs of Inigo Jones and William Kent. John Vardy, London, 1744.

Waite, John G. and Paul R. Huey
Northwest Stonehouse, Johnson Hall a Historic Structure Report. New York State Historic Trust, New York, 1971.

Wallace, Arthur W.
An Album of Drawings of Early Buildings in Nova-Scotia. Heritage Trust of Nova Scotia, Halifax, 1976.

Ware, Isaac
A Complete Body of Architecture Adorned with Plans and Elevations from Original Designs.... T. Osborne and J. Shepton, London, 1756.
—. The Four Books of Andrea Palladio's Architecture: Wherein After a Short Treatise of the Five Orders Those Observations that are the Most Necessary in Building.... Isaac Ware, London, 1738.
—. The Plans, Elevations and Sections; Chimney Pieces and Ceilings of Houghton in Norfolk.... Isaac Ware London, 1735.

Weld, Isaac
Travels Through the States of North America and the Provinces of Upper and Lower Canada During the Years 1795, 1796 and 1797. 4th

ed., John Stockdale, London, 1807, 2 vols.

Whiffen, Marcus
American Architecture since 1780. A Guide to the Styles. MIT Press, Cambridge, 1969.
——. Stuart and Georgian Churches; the Architecture of the Church of England Outside London, 1603-1837. Batsford, London, 1948.

Wittkower, Rufolf
Architectural Principles in the Age of Humanism. Reprint 4th ed. 1973, Academy Editions, London, 1974.
——. Art and Architecture in Italy 1600-1750. Penguin, Harmondsworth, 1965.
——. Palladio and English Palladianism. Thames and Hudson, London, ca. 1974.

Woolwich, Royal Military Academy
Records of the Royal Military Academy 1741-1892. F.J. Cattermole, Woolwich, 1892.

Wright, Janet
"Domestic Architecture of the Picturesque in Canada: Villas and Cottages Suitable for Persons of Genteel Life and Moderate Fortune." Manuscript on file, National Historic Parks and Sites Branch, Parks Canada, Ottawa, 1980. (Forthcoming publication, "Architecture of the Picturesque in Canada," Studies in Archaeology, Architecture and History, Parks Canada, Ottawa, 1984.)

———. "Palladio's Typology in Relation to the Double Loggia Design." Term paper, Queen's University, Jan. 1977.

Würtele, F.C.
"The English Cathedral of Quebec." Transactions of the Literary and Historical Society of Quebec. No. 20 (1889-91, 1891), pp. 76-84. Quebec.